Microsoft® Office Outlook® 2016: Part 1 (Desktop/ Office 365™)

Microsoft® Office Outlook® 2016: Part 1 (Desktop/Office 365™)

Part Number: 091058
Course Edition: 3.0

Acknowledgements

PROJECT TEAM

Author	Media Designer	Content Editor
Laurie A. Perry	Brian Sullivan	Michelle Farney

Logical Operations wishes to thank the Logical Operations Instructor Community, and in particular Thomas Allen and Joe Valentine, for contributing their instructional and technical expertise during the creation of this course.

Notices

DISCLAIMER

While Logical Operations, Inc. takes care to ensure the accuracy and quality of these materials, we cannot guarantee their accuracy, and all materials are provided without any warranty whatsoever, including, but not limited to, the implied warranties of merchantability or fitness for a particular purpose. The name used in the data files for this course is that of a fictitious company. Any resemblance to current or future companies is purely coincidental. We do not believe we have used anyone's name in creating this course, but if we have, please notify us and we will change the name in the next revision of the course. Logical Operations is an independent provider of integrated training solutions for individuals, businesses, educational institutions, and government agencies. The use of screenshots, photographs of another entity's products, or another entity's product name or service in this book is for editorial purposes only. No such use should be construed to imply sponsorship or endorsement of the book by nor any affiliation of such entity with Logical Operations. This courseware may contain links to sites on the Internet that are owned and operated by third parties (the "External Sites"). Logical Operations is not responsible for the availability of, or the content located on or through, any External Site. Please contact Logical Operations if you have any concerns regarding such links or External Sites.

TRADEMARK NOTICES

Microsoft® Office Outlook® 2016: Part 1 (Desktop/Office 365™)

About This Course

Email has become one of the most widely used methods of communication, whether for personal or business communications. In most organizations, large or small, email is the preferred form of communicating information amongst employees. As email grows in popularity and use, most organizations have found the need to implement a corporate mail management system such as Microsoft® Office Outlook® to handle the messages and meeting invitations sent among employees.

In this course, you will use Outlook to send, receive, and manage email messages, manage your contact information, schedule appointments and meetings, create tasks and notes for yourself, and customize the Outlook interface to suit your working style.

This course is the first in a series of two Microsoft® Office Outlook® 2016 courses. It will provide you with the basic skills you need to start using Outlook 2016 to manage your email communications, contact information, calendar events, tasks, and notes.

You can also use this course to prepare for the Microsoft Office Specialist (MOS) Certification exams for Microsoft Outlook 2016.

Course Description

Target Student

This course is intended for people who have a basic understanding of Microsoft® Windows® and need to know how to use Outlook as an email client to manage their email communications, calendar appointments, contact information, and other communication tasks. In addition to creating and sending email, this course will introduce you to organizing your mail, working with attachments, formatting message text, scheduling meetings, and responding to meeting invitations.

Course Prerequisites

To ensure your success in this course you should have end-user skills with any current version of Windows, including being able to start and close applications, navigate basic file structures, and manage files and folders is recommended. You can obtain this level of skill and knowledge by taking either one of the following Logical Operations courses, or any similar course in general Microsoft Windows skills:

- *Using Microsoft® Windows® 10*
- *Microsoft® Windows® 10: Transition from Windows® 7*

Course Objectives

In this course, you will use Outlook to manage your email communications, including composing, reading, and responding to emails; schedule appointments and meetings;

manage contact information; schedule tasks and create notes; customize message response options; and organize your mail.

You will:

- Navigate Outlook 2016 to read and respond to email.
- Use the Address Book, and format and spell check new messages.
- Attach files and insert illustrations to messages.
- Customize read and response options.
- Use flags, categories, and folders to organize messages.
- Create and work with Contacts.
- Create appointments and schedule meetings in Calendar.
- Create and work with Tasks and Notes.

The CHOICE Home Screen

Logon and access information for your CHOICE environment will be provided with your class experience. The CHOICE platform is your entry point to the CHOICE learning experience, of which this course manual is only one part.

On the CHOICE Home screen, you can access the CHOICE Course screens for your specific courses. Visit the CHOICE Course screen both during and after class to make use of the world of support and instructional resources that make up the CHOICE experience.

Each CHOICE Course screen will give you access to the following resources:

- **Classroom**: A link to your training provider's classroom environment.
- **eBook**: An interactive electronic version of the printed book for your course.
- **Files**: Any course files available to download.
- **Checklists**: Step-by-step procedures and general guidelines you can use as a reference during and after class.
- **LearnTOs**: Brief animated videos that enhance and extend the classroom learning experience.
- **Assessment**: A course assessment for your self-assessment of the course content.
- Social media resources that enable you to collaborate with others in the learning community using professional communications sites such as LinkedIn or microblogging tools such as Twitter.

Depending on the nature of your course and the components chosen by your learning provider, the CHOICE Course screen may also include access to elements such as:

- LogicalLABS, a virtual technical environment for your course.
- Various partner resources related to the courseware.
- Related certifications or credentials.
- A link to your training provider's website.
- Notices from the CHOICE administrator.
- Newsletters and other communications from your learning provider.
- Mentoring services.

Visit your CHOICE Home screen often to connect, communicate, and extend your learning experience!

How to Use This Book

As You Learn

This book is divided into lessons and topics, covering a subject or a set of related subjects. In most cases, lessons are arranged in order of increasing proficiency.

The results-oriented topics include relevant and supporting information you need to master the content. Each topic has various types of activities designed to enable you to solidify your understanding of the informational material presented in the course. Information is provided for reference and reflection to facilitate understanding and practice.

Data files for various activities as well as other supporting files for the course are available by download from the CHOICE Course screen. In addition to sample data for the course exercises, the course files may contain media components to enhance your learning and additional reference materials for use both during and after the course.

Checklists of procedures and guidelines can be used during class and as after-class references when you're back on the job and need to refresh your understanding.

At the back of the book, you will find a glossary of the definitions of the terms and concepts used throughout the course. You will also find an index to assist in locating information within the instructional components of the book.

As You Review

Any method of instruction is only as effective as the time and effort you, the student, are willing to invest in it. In addition, some of the information that you learn in class may not be important to you immediately, but it may become important later. For this reason, we encourage you to spend some time reviewing the content of the course after your time in the classroom.

As a Reference

The organization and layout of this book make it an easy-to-use resource for future reference. Taking advantage of the glossary, index, and table of contents, you can use this book as a first source of definitions, background information, and summaries.

Course Icons

Watch throughout the material for the following visual cues.

Icon	Description
	A **Note** provides additional information, guidance, or hints about a topic or task.
	A **Caution** note makes you aware of places where you need to be particularly careful with your actions, settings, or decisions so that you can be sure to get the desired results of an activity or task.
	LearnTO notes show you where an associated LearnTO is particularly relevant to the content. Access LearnTOs from your CHOICE Course screen.
	Checklists provide job aids you can use after class as a reference to perform skills back on the job. Access checklists from your CHOICE Course screen.
	Social notes remind you to check your CHOICE Course screen for opportunities to interact with the CHOICE community using social media.

1 Getting Started with Outlook 2016

Lesson Time: 45 minutes

Lesson Objectives

In this lesson, you will:

- Navigate the Outlook interface.

- Read, respond, delete, and print messages.

- Access Outlook Help.

Lesson Introduction

To be successful in Microsoft® Office Outlook® 2016, you need to know how to navigate the interface and know how to perform basic email functions like creating and sending an email, reading and responding to an email, and even printing or deleting an email. Additionally, if you find yourself needing some assistance while using the interface, you need to know how to use the Outlook Help tool to provide you with the necessary information. Knowing the interface and how to use its components will enable you to perform any of the basic email functions that will be required of you in an email-friendly work environment.

TOPIC A

Navigate the Outlook Interface

Knowing how to navigate within the Outlook interface and how all of the components of the application function will help you become familiar with the ins and outs of the Outlook environment before you even begin working with the application. When you are comfortable and familiar with the tool and how it works, you will be able to easily use the application to begin sending and receiving emails.

Email

Email, or electronic mail, refers to electronic mail messages that can be delivered and exchanged between one sender and one or more recipients. Email messages are nearly immediate in nature; depending on the size of the email and barring any technical errors in delivery, an email message is received immediately upon being sent. It is then dependent on the recipients to read and respond to the message as needed or as they see fit. Email is one of the most common methods of communication being used for instances when multiple people need to be involved in a single conversation and a response is needed in a timely manner. For this reason, email is growing quickly in both the business world and in personal communications as the preferred method of communication.

Email Clients

In order to send and receive email messages, an email client is needed. The email client is an application that is used to access, display, and interact with the electronic messages.

Email Addresses

Email messages are sent from one email address to another. An email address is a string of information that specifies a person and place to send the message to. An email address is made up of three parts:

- The local part, which is a unique user name made up of alphabetic and numeric characters, and possibly special characters like an underscore.
- The @ symbol immediately after the local part.
- The domain part, which is a hostname and a standard extension such as .com or .net.

The local part   The domain part

Dietrich.Brown@develetech.example

Figure 1–1: An email address.

Microsoft Outlook 2016

Microsoft Outlook 2016 is the email client that is provided with the Microsoft Office 2016 suite of products. Using Outlook 2016, you can compose and work with email messages and the information included with those messages. This includes reading and responding to emails. In addition to email, Outlook provides features to manage your contact information, schedule meetings and appointments, and keep track of tasks.

- **Mail**
- **Contacts**
- **Calendar**
- **Tasks**
- **Notes**

Outlook

Figure 1-2: Outlook 2016.

There are several ways for you to purchase Outlook 2016. Traditionally, the desktop application was purchased from a brick-and-mortar store and then installed onto your computer from CDs. Now, the common practice is to purchase the Office suite of products through an Office 365 subscription. With Office 365 login credentials, you have access to download and install Office 2016 on your desktop, which includes Outlook 2016.

In addition to the desktop versions of the Office applications, you can also download mobile app versions of the Office suite from the Microsoft Store. These mobile apps provide most of the same functionality as the desktop versions and they require only an Internet connection. With the mobile apps, you can work with your Office apps and data from anywhere at any time.

> **Note: Outlook on the Web**
>
> Through your Office 365™ subscription, you have access to the Outlook on the Web app. Throughout this course, you will see notes that identify any significant differences between the desktop application and the online app.

Office Online Apps

When you purchase an Office 365 subscription, you also have access to the Office Online apps which include Microsoft® Excel®, Microsoft® Word, Microsoft® PowerPoint®, Outlook, and a variety of other apps. You can use any web browser to access Office 365 by navigating to **login.microsoftonline.com** and signing in with your Office 365 user account and password. These online apps are scaled-down versions of the Office 2016 desktop applications and provide basic features and some of the same functionality that exists in the desktop applications. The advantage of using the Office Online apps is the ability to access, edit, share, and store your online files across a variety of devices.

Items and Folders

You will interact with items and folders, which are two basic elements in Outlook.

- *Items* in Outlook contain the information that you are viewing or working with. Items include email messages, calendar entries, contact information, tasks, and notes.
- *Folders* are the organizational containers in which items in Outlook are stored. Folders are most often used to organize your email messages. Some folders are included as defaults with an Outlook installation to help manage your mail, including the **Inbox**, **Drafts**, **Sent Items**, **Deleted Items**, **Outbox**, **RSS Feeds**, and **Search Folders** folders. New folders can be created to group items that are related to one another and help you easily find and manage your Outlook items.

Components of the Outlook Interface

There are a number of standard components that make up the Outlook 2016 interface.

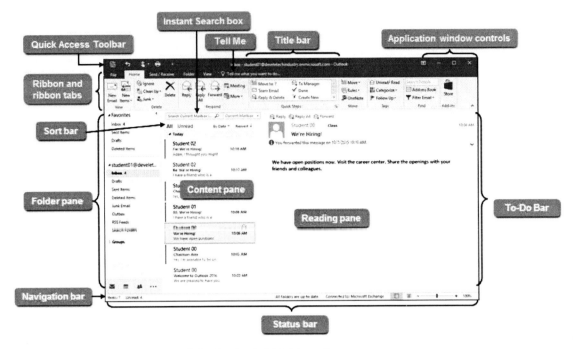

Figure 1-3: The components of the Outlook 2016 interface.

Component	Description
Title bar	Located at the very top of the window, the **Title bar** displays the title of the folder where you are currently located, the name of the email account you are viewing, and the name of the application (Microsoft Outlook).
Application window controls	Located in the upper-right corner of the application window, these buttons are used to show/hide the ribbon, minimize the window, maximize the window, or close the application.
Quick Access Toolbar	Located in the upper-left corner of the window, it displays a number of commands that are commonly used within the interface, providing easy access to these tools.
Ribbon and ribbon tabs	Located below the **Title bar** in the window, the ribbon is comprised of multiple tabs that each contain buttons and commands used to perform actions within the Outlook interface. The tabs and the buttons contained on each tab are grouped by function.
Tell Me	Located to the right of the ribbon tabs, this new feature is used to search for a specific action, to access online help documents, or to access the **Smart Lookup** pane.
Folder pane	Located on the left side of the window, it displays all of the folders available in the Outlook environment for the email account you are viewing, including the Inbox for the account. You can customize which folders are displayed and the order in which they are listed.
Content pane	Located in the middle of the Outlook window, it displays all of the individual items within the specific folder in which you are located. For instance, when the **Inbox** folder is selected, the **Content** pane displays the message list of the messages currently in the Inbox. The contents of this pane will change to reflect the currently selected folder or Outlook item.

Component	Description
Sort bar	Located above the item list in the **Content** pane, it displays the titles of all the columns that are currently being shown for your Outlook items, and can be used to arrange or sort how the items are displayed in the pane (sorted by subject, sorted by size, and more).
Instant Search box	Located at the top of the **Content** pane, the **Instant Search** box, is used to enter a term or keyword, and searches your Outlook items for instances of that term. It then displays the resulting items that contain that term somewhere in their contents.
Reading pane	Located at the right side of the Outlook window, it displays the contents of the Outlook item you have currently selected, such as the contents of an email message you have selected in the **Content** pane for the Inbox. It provides a preview of the contents of the item before it is opened in a separate Outlook window.
To-Do Bar	By default, the **To-Do Bar** is not displayed in Outlook 2016. When displayed, you can choose to show Calendar, People, or Tasks content on the far right side of the Outlook window.
Navigation bar	Located below the **Folder** pane, it displays launch buttons for the other Outlook views like the Calendar, People, and Tasks views. By default, the buttons are displayed in Compact view as small icons.
Status bar	Located along the bottom of the Outlook window, it displays information related to the currently selected folder, such as the number of items in the folder, if the folder is up-to-date or is currently sending or receiving information, and more.

Note: Throughout this course you will be introduced to ways in which you can customize your Outlook environment. The next course in the series, *Microsoft® Office Outlook® 2016: Part 2* provides an in-depth look at customizing the Outlook environment.

Note: Outlook on the Web

The online app user interface is noticeably scaled down from the desktop application. The **Quick Access Toolbar** is not available in the online app, and instead of the **Navigation bar**, you use the **App Launcher** icon to access the tiles for **Calendar**, **People**, and **Tasks**.

The Ribbon

The *ribbon* is a component of the Outlook 2016 user interface (UI) that is also shared by all Microsoft Office 2016 applications. Displayed along the top of the Outlook window, the ribbon provides quick access to frequently used commands that are organized by tabs that contain command groups. These command groups contain sets of functionally-related commands that you will use to create and send email messages, schedule calendar events, and basically work in Outlook.

Note: This course uses a streamlined notation for ribbon commands. They'll appear as "[Ribbon Tab]→[Group]→[Button or Control]" as in "Select **Home**→**New**→**New Email**." If the group name isn't needed for navigation or there isn't a group, it's omitted, as in "Select **File**→**Open**." For selections that open menus and submenus, this notation convention will continue until you are directed to select the final command or option, as in "Select **View**→**Layout**→**Reading Pane**→**Bottom**."

Some ribbon groups also display a *dialog box launcher*. These downward-facing arrows in the bottom-right corner of some command groups open dialog boxes that provide you with access to even more commands and options related to the functionality of the particular group's commands.

Figure 1-4: The components of the ribbon in Outlook 2016.

The following table provides a description of the various ribbon elements.

Ribbon Element	Description
Tabs	Organize the ribbon at the highest level according to task functions such as sending and receiving with email, managing folders, and changing the view.
Groups	Contain functionally related sets of commands used to perform most Outlook tasks.
Commands	Execute the desired action or configure the desired settings and options.
Dialog box launchers	Open dialog boxes containing further commands or options related to the functionality of the group's commands.
Tell Me text box	Enables you to perform a keyword search for Outlook commands and to access help topics.

Note: Outlook on the Web

Unlike the desktop app, the online app has a **command bar** instead of the familiar ribbon. This is a scaled-down version of the full desktop application's ribbon and the commands are specific to the selected window component. For example, if a message is selected, the **Delete, Archive, Move to** and **Categories** commands appear. If a folder is selected, then you will see the **Empty folder** command.

Note: The ribbon is a feature of all products in the Office 2016 suite. For more information, check out the LearnTO **Navigate the Office 2016 Ribbon** presentation from the **LearnTO** tile on the CHOICE Course screen.

Outlook Ribbon Tabs

There are five default ribbon tabs in Outlook. Each provides access to the commands within the tab that perform an action.

Ribbon Tab	Description
File	The **File** tab provides access to the **Backstage** view where you manage features and properties of either the Outlook application or perform actions on the active Outlook item. Item-specific tasks include saving attachments and printing. General environment-related tasks include configuring settings for the active account and modifying Outlook options.

Ribbon Tab	Description
Home	The commands displayed on the **Home** tab will vary depending on whether you are working in the Outlook window or within an active item. Each Outlook item will display different command groups that are specific to the actions needed for that item. The **Home** tab may display a different title for some types of items when the item is active in a new window: **Message** for emails, **Appointment** or **Meeting** for calendar entries, **Contact** for contact entries, and **Task** for tasks.
Send/Receive	The **Send/Receive** tab displays commands specific to synchronizing, sending, and receiving data for Outlook items. It also includes commands to download items and work offline.
Folder	The **Folder** tab displays commands used to create, move, delete, and generally manage any folders in the Outlook environment. There are also commands available for managing folder contents, organizing folders, and setting folder properties.
View	The **View** tab displays commands used for setting or adjusting the layout of the Outlook window and how items are displayed within the window.

ScreenTips

When you hover your cursor over a command icon or button in the Outlook window, a small window with descriptive text will appear. These text windows are called *ScreenTips*, and they provide information about what action the command or button performs.

The Backstage View

The **Backstage** view is a feature provided in all Microsoft Office products and offers a single location to manage features and properties of either the Outlook application or the current active item. You access the **Backstage** view by selecting the **File** tab in the window.

When launched for the application, the **Backstage** view displays the **Account Information** page on the **Info** tab by default. From the **Account Information** page, you can manage your Outlook account, including modifying account settings, enabling automatic replies, or using the mailbox cleanup tools. You can also open other calendars or data files, import or export files, print items, manage your Office Account, access the **Outlook Options** dialog box, or exit the application.

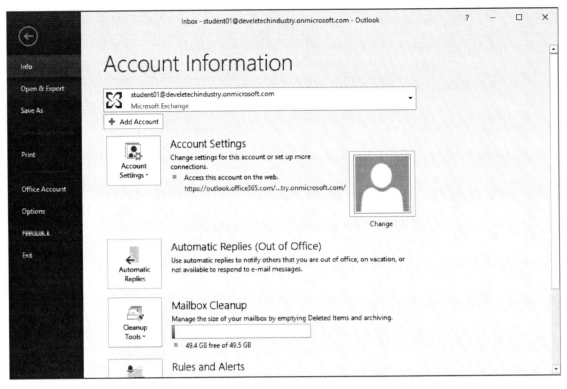

Figure 1-5: The Backstage view in Outlook 2016.

When you open an Outlook item in a separate window and then select the **File** tab, the **Backstage** view displays information, options, and properties specific to the selected item. Some of the available options include viewing the properties for the item, managing the location of the item, and for mail messages, managing permissions and other settings. You can also save items or attachments, print the active item, close the active item, manage your Office Account, or access the **Outlook Options** dialog box.

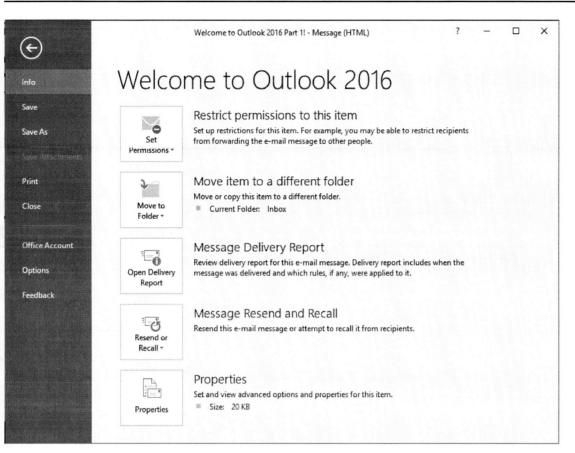

Figure 1-6: The Backstage view for an email message in Outlook.

	Note: Outlook on the Web
	Instead of a **Backstage** view, the buttons at the far right end of the command bar can be used to control Outlook settings and access account information. You can access and configure notifications, Outlook options, help, and your account settings.

Mail View

The **Mail** view is the default view in the Outlook environment. The **Mail** view is where you work with the email messages that you create and send, as well as the ones that you receive. All of your email messages and some other Outlook items are stored in the various mail folders in Outlook. These folders appear in the **Folder** pane of the Outlook window.

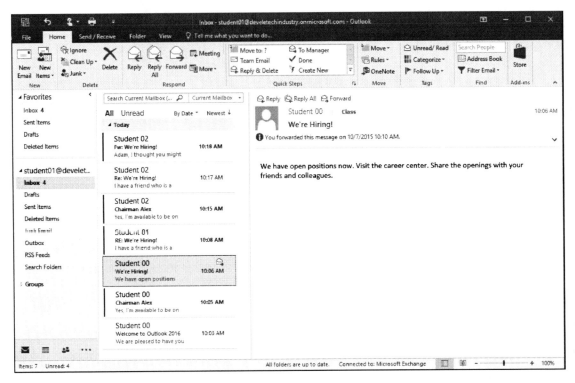

Figure 1-7: The Mail view in Outlook 2016.

Note: Outlook on the Web

In the online app, your mail is displayed in a scaled-down version of the desktop application **Mail** view that is shown here. The **Folder** pane, message list, search field, and **Reading** pane function in a similar manner. Instead of the ribbon running horizontally across the top of the window, you will see the Office 365 header with the **App Launcher** icon at the far left and icons to access notifications, application settings, and help at the far right end.

Mail Folders

The following are the default folders in Outlook.

Mail Folder	Description
Inbox	By default, the **Inbox** folder is opened when Outlook is launched. The Inbox displays all of the email messages and meeting invitations or responses that have been received by the user. The items in the Inbox are displayed in the **View** pane in the Outlook interface, and the contents of the selected or active item is displayed in the **Reading** pane.
Drafts	The **Drafts** folder stores copies of email messages that are in progress of being composed, or have been composed and not sent. You can access these unfinished messages in the folder at a later time to be completed and sent.
Sent Items	The **Sent Items** folder stores copies of Outlook items that you have previously sent, including email messages, meeting invites, and meeting responses. By default, items that you send are stored in the **Sent Items** folder, though you can configure these items to be saved to an alternative location.
Deleted Items	The **Deleted Items** folder stores all of the Outlook items that you have deleted from other folders.

Mail Folder	Description
Clutter	The **Clutter** folder stores all your low-priority messages. As you move selected messages to this folder, Outlook keeps track of your preferences and automatically moves similar messages to your **Clutter** folder. This process usually takes a few days to begin, and even then, Outlook might not be completely accurate.
Conversation History	The **Conversation History** folder stores your instant message chats.
Junk Email	The **Junk EMail** folder stores any email messages from unknown or untrusted senders that appear to be spam or junk mail.
Outbox	The **Outbox** folder temporarily stores email messages that have been sent while they are in the process of being delivered to the recipient.
RSS Subscriptions	The **RSS Feeds** folder is used to access the items from websites you have subscribed to using a Real Simple Syndication (RSS) feed.
Search Folders	The **Search Folders** folder is used to access any search folders you have created in Outlook to search for specific keywords or phrases.

Read and Unread Messages

Outlook visually differentiates the messages in your Message list that are read or unread. If a message is unread, the subject line displays in blue, bold font and a vertical blue bar appears on the left side of the message in the Message list. Once the message has been selected and viewed, even in the **Reading** pane, the blue bar and blue, bold font in the subject line no longer appear to indicate that the message has been read.

Note: When the **Reading** pane is displayed to the right of the Outlook window, as it does by default, both the blue bar and the blue, bold font display to denote an unread message. If you choose to display the **Reading** pane at the bottom of the Outlook window, the blue bar is not displayed; only the blue, bold font identifies unread messages.

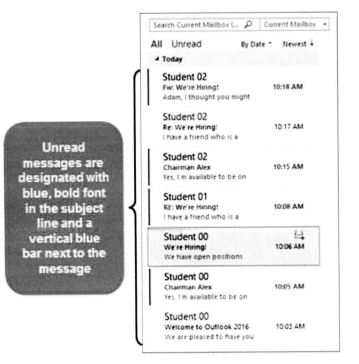

Figure 1-8: Unread messages in the message list.

Message Icons

One or more message icons may appear in association with the messages in the Inbox. Each icon conveys information about that particular Outlook message that may help you react to and manage your email messages appropriately. There are a few icons that are commonly seen in relation to email messages.

Keep in mind that you won't necessarily see all of the available icons in your Inbox; some icons don't apply to your items unless you have activated settings or options within the environment.

Icon	Description
	Replied To: The email message was replied to.
	Forwarded: The email message has been forwarded.
!	**High Importance:** The email message contains important and potentially time-sensitive information, and should be read or/and replied to as soon as possible.
	Attachment: The email contains an attached document.
	Flagged for Follow Up: This email has been flagged by you for follow up. The flag icon serves as a reminder that you need to follow up with an action or a response to this email by a certain date or time.

Note: There are other icons that you may see in your Inbox regarding other Outlook tools, such as **Calendar** or **Tasks**. More information is available about those icons where those tools are covered in this course.

Calendar View

The **Calendar** view is used for scheduling and managing any personal or professional events that you are participating in.

The **Calendar** view contains two main components: the **Folder** pane and the calendar grid. The **Folder** pane displays the calendar for the current month and the following month, and provides navigation through the months of the year. When a date is selected on the calendar, it displays in the calendar grid. The default view for the calendar grid is the **Month** view, which displays the entire month, with the current date highlighted. Any appointments or meetings scheduled throughout the month will display on the appropriate day in the calendar.

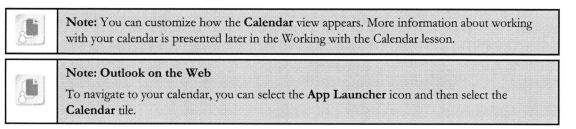

Figure 1-9: The Calendar view in Outlook 2016.

> **Note:** You can customize how the **Calendar** view appears. More information about working with your calendar is presented later in the Working with the Calendar lesson.

> **Note: Outlook on the Web**
>
> To navigate to your calendar, you can select the **App Launcher** icon and then select the **Calendar** tile.

Contacts View

The **Contacts** view is used to create and manage your own personal address book of people with whom you communicate on a regular basis.

The **Contacts** view contains three main components, from left to right: the **Folder** pane displays your folders, the **Content** pane displays your contacts, and the **Reading** pane displays the selected contact's information. By default, your contacts are displayed in **People** view where you can edit existing contacts, create new contacts, create new contact groups, and quickly perform an action such as email a selected contact.

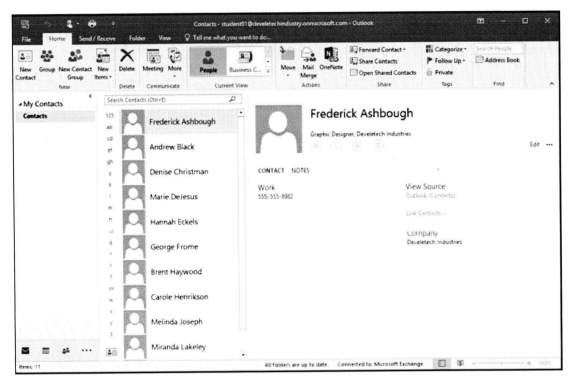

Figure 1-10: The Contacts view in Outlook 2016.

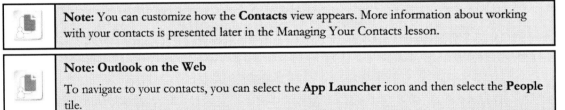

Note: You can customize how the **Contacts** view appears. More information about working with your contacts is presented later in the Managing Your Contacts lesson.

Note: Outlook on the Web

To navigate to your contacts, you can select the **App Launcher** icon and then select the **People** tile.

Tasks View

The **Tasks** view is used for creating and managing personal tasks that need to be completed. You can assign tasks to yourself or other people. Tasks assigned to you will also appear in your **To-Do** list. The **Tasks** view contains three main components: the **Folder** pane displays your task folders, the **Content** pane displays the list of tasks, and the **Reading** pane displays the details of the selected task.

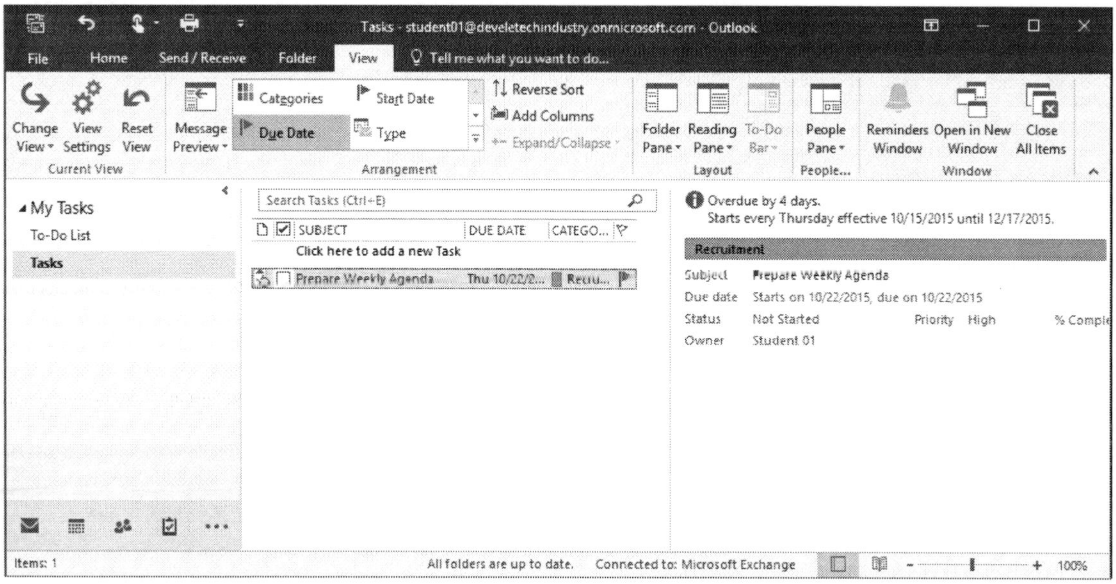

Figure 1-11: Tasks view in Outlook 2016.

Note: Outlook on the Web

To navigate to your tasks, you can select the **App Launcher** icon and then select the **Tasks** tile.

Notes View

The Notes feature is used to keep track of project and personal information. **Notes** allow you to capture important information that you don't want to forget or lose track of and save within your Outlook environment. When you visit the **Notes** section, you can view all of the notes you have created for yourself. You can also assign categories and category colors to easily identify your Notes. You can access your Notes by selecting the **Notes** icon in the **Navigation** bar.

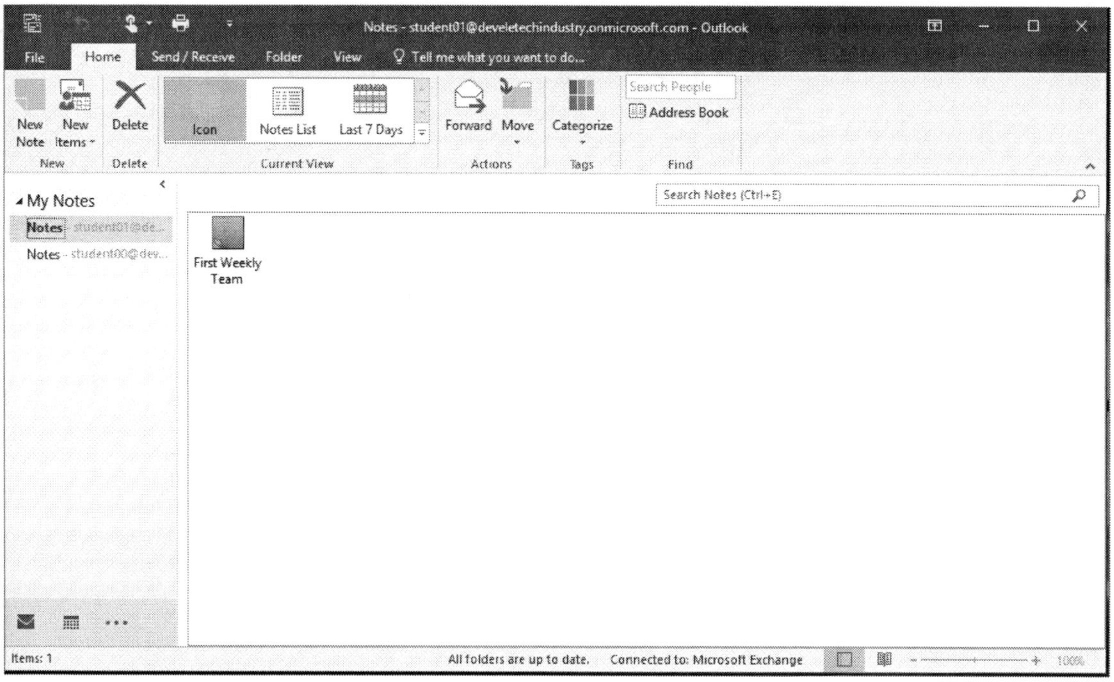

Figure 1-12: The Notes view.

> **Note: Outlook on the Web**
>
> In the online app, your notes are contained in the **Notes** folder in your Mail window.

Peeks

The *peeks* feature in Outlook allows you to see a preview of your other views without having to leave the active view. For instance, if you are in the **Mail** view, but want to get a quick idea of any upcoming calendar events, you can hover over the **Calendar** button in the **Navigation** bar and Outlook will display a peek of your calendar information. You can view a quick peek of your Calendar, People, and Tasks.

If you'd prefer to keep the peek always visible on screen, you can dock it by selecting the **Dock the peek** button in the upper-right corner of the peek. When you do this, the peek is docked in the **To-Do Bar** along the rightmost side of the Outlook window.

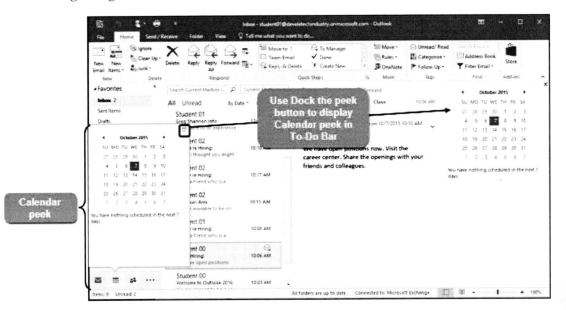
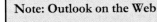
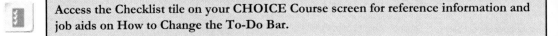

Figure 1-13: The Calendar peeks as a pop-up and docked.

> **Note: Outlook on the Web**
>
> Because the **Navigation bar** is not a component of the online app, this feature is also not available. To switch between your mail, calendar, contacts, and tasks, you will use the **App Launcher** icon and the associated tiles.

> **Access the Checklist tile on your CHOICE Course screen for reference information and job aids on How to Change the To-Do Bar.**

ACTIVITY 1–1
Navigating the Outlook 2016 Interface

Before You Begin

Your instructor has sent you a Welcome email message.

Scenario

You work for Develetech Industries, a mid-sized company that designs and manufactures home electronics. Develetech has just rolled out Outlook 2016 as its new email application. Before you begin using Outlook to communicate via email, it is a good idea to familiarize yourself with the Outlook interface and its components.

 Note: Activities may vary slightly if the software vendor has issued digital updates. Your instructor will notify you of any changes.

---

1. Launch Outlook 2016.

   a) Select and select **All apps**.
   b) From the list of apps, select **Outlook 2016**.

   > **Note:** If Outlook 2016 has been pinned to the taskbar, then you can launch Outlook from the taskbar icon.

   c) Select the **Maximize** button to expand the Outlook window.

2. Explore the **Mail** view.

   a) In the **Content** pane, select the "Welcome" message from your instructor.

   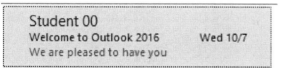

   Student 00
   Welcome to Outlook 2016   Wed 10/7
   We are pleased to have you

   b) In the **Reading** pane, view the message body.
   c) Select the other default folders in the **Folder** pane to view their contents.
      Your Favorites are listed at the top of the pane. All other folders are listed under your account name. Except for the Inbox, the folders are empty at this point.
   d) Select the **Inbox** folder and observe the ribbon at the top of the screen.
   e) On the **Home** tab, view the command groups and available buttons displayed on it.
      The command buttons are divided into command groups based on their function. Some command buttons initiate a command, such as the **New Email** button. Other command buttons contain a list of additional commands to choose from, as indicated by the drop-down arrow.

---

f) Press the **Alt** key.

The **Alt** key enables you to activate a ribbon tab by typing the display keyboard key.

g) Press **Alt** again or select a blank area of the screen to hide the keyboard shortcuts.

3. Add the **Print** command to the **Quick Access Toolbar**.

a) View the icons currently displaying in the **Quick Access Toolbar** at the top-left corner of the screen.

By default, three commands are visible: **Send/Receive All Folders**, **Undo**, and **Touch/Mouse Mode**.

b) On the **Quick Access Toolbar**, select the **Customize Quick Access Toolbar** drop-down arrow. You can show or hide command buttons by selecting them from this list.

c) Select **Print**.

4. View the available components of the **To-Do Bar** and how they appear when enabled.

a) Select the **View** tab and in the **Layout** command group, select **To-Do Bar** to view the available components.

You can display details from Calendar, Contacts, and Tasks in the right-most pane in of the **Mail** view.

b) Select **Calendar** to display a monthly calendar with a list of scheduled events below it.

c) Select **To-Do Bar→Off**.

5. Explore the **Calendar** view.

a) In the **Navigation** bar, select **Calendar**.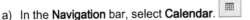
By default, the Calendar opens in **Month** view. The **Folder** pane contains two miniature monthly calendars for the current month and the following one.

b) In the **Folder** pane, select a date sometime next week.

When you select a different day in the **Folder** pane, the Calendar changes to the **Day** view for the selected day. On the ribbon, in the **Arrange** command group, **Day** is selected to indicate that it's the current view.

c) On the **Home** tab, use the buttons in the **Arrange** command group to change the display of the Calendar.

d) Select **Month** to return the view to the default view.

e) Select the **View** tab to observe the available commands.

> **Note:** Notice how the command groups and commands are different on the ribbon tabs for the **Calendar** than those that appeared in the **Mail** view.

6. Explore the **Contacts** view.

a) In the **Navigation** bar, select **People.**
By default, there are no contacts in Outlook. However, the contacts you see have been added by your instructor prior to class.

b) On the ribbon tabs, view the contact-related commands.

7. Explore the **Tasks** view.

a) In the **Navigation** bar, select **Tasks.**

The **Folder** pane contains both the To-Do List and Tasks items. A task item is an Outlook item that you create to keep track of events and tasks you need to accomplish. The To-Do List contains your tasks and any messages or contacts that you've flagged for further action.

b) On the ribbon, view the task-related commands.
The **Home** tab reflects the active view and provides the appropriate command buttons.

8. Explore the **Backstage** view.

a) Select the **File** tab.

b) Observe the **Backstage** view.

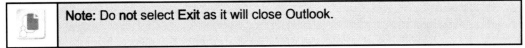

The **Backstage** view provides a single location to manage general Outlook settings, as well as print selected items, export files, and provide feedback to Microsoft.

> **Note:** Do **not** select **Exit** as it will close Outlook.

9. Close the **Backstage** view and return to the **Mail** view.

a) Select the button. ⊖

b) In the **Navigation** bar, select the **Mail** icon. ✉

TOPIC B

Work with Messages

Now that you are familiar with the Outlook environment, you are ready to start communicating with others. In this topic, you will perform basic Outlook mail functions, such as creating and sending messages, reading and responding to messages, and printing and deleting messages to begin using Outlook as a communication tool.

The Message Form

The message form is the window that is launched in Outlook when you create a new email or respond to an email. In the message form, you will:

- Add your primary recipients in the **To** field and any secondary recipients to be copied on the message in the **Cc** field.
- Add the subject matter or purpose of the email in the **Subject** field.
- Add the content of your message in the message body.

> **Note:** The **Bcc** and **From** fields do not automatically display in the message form window, but can be added to the message form optionally.

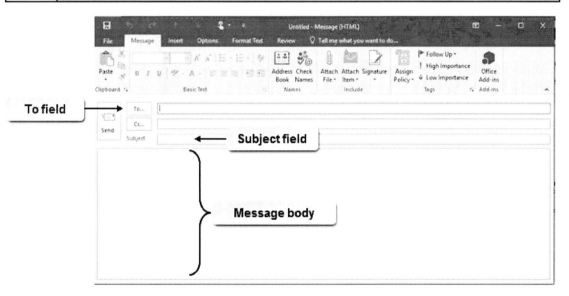

Figure 1-14: The message form in Outlook.

Cc vs. Bcc

Recipients included in the **Cc** (carbon copy) field will receive a copy of the email message, and will be visible as a recipient of the message. Recipients included in the **Bcc** (blind carbon copy) field will receive a copy of the message, but they are invisible to the other recipients as being included on the message.

> **Note: Outlook on the Web**
>
> When you select the **New** button, a new message appears on the right side of the window instead of in a separate own window. Unlike the message form in the desktop application, the available commands and options are slightly scaled back.

Message Form Tabs

The ribbon in the new Untitled message window displays tabs and command groups that provide specific options and features to use when composing an email.

Figure 1-15: The ribbon and tabs on a message form.

Message Form Tab	Description
File	Opens the **Backstage** view for the current email message. The **Info** section of the **Backstage** view for the message provides a location where you can set permissions and advanced properties for the message, if needed or desired.
Message	Provides actions and options for basic email functions, such as using the clipboard, formatting text, attaching files or signatures, and tagging messages with follow-up options or priority levels.
Insert	Provides actions and options for inserting various objects into your email message, such as including an Outlook item or inserting tables, illustrations, links, text, or symbols.
Options	Provides actions and options for enhancing your email with more advanced features, including adding a theme, displaying hidden fields, setting permissions, using tracking features, and other options related to message delivery.
Format Text	Provides actions and options for common text formatting, such as using the clipboard, changing the text format, modifying the font and paragraph formatting, and applying styles.
Review	Provides actions and options for reviewing your email for proper grammar and usage before sending, such as using proofing tools like spell check or the thesaurus, and implementing language tools, if necessary.

ACTIVITY 1-2
Creating and Sending an Email

Scenario

Develetech is growing and hiring many new employees. You have been asked to be part of a team working on a recruitment plan and the hiring process. You heard that your coworker, Alex Jaffey, will be the chairman of the team. You want to send a quick email to Alex to confirm your involvement in the project.

---

1. Create a new email that is addressed to everyone in class.
   a) On the **Home** tab, select **New Email**.

   b) In the **To** field, type the email address of another student in the class as
   student##@[your_domain.com]

   > **Note:** When Outlook recognizes the email address, the displayed name changes to reflect that name recognition.

   c) Type a semicolon *;*
   d) Type the second student email address.
   e) Continue to add the email addresses of all students. Be sure to separate them with semicolons.

2. Complete the message with a subject of **Chairman Alex** and the message that follows.
   a) In the **Subject** field, type *Chairman Alex*
   b) In the message body, type *Yes, I'm available to be on the recruitment team for the graphic design hires.*

   > **Note:** It's not necessary to type the text verbatim. You can type the text of your choice rather than the indicated text.

3. Send the email.
   a) Select **Send** to send the message.

Message Response Options

When you receive an email in Outlook and need to respond to the message, there are a number of reply options that you can choose from when responding. If the message has been opened in a separate window, then the Reply options are located in the **Respond** command group on the **Message** tab. These options include:

- **Reply** to create a response email where the recipient is only the sender of the initial email.
- **Reply All** to create a response email where the recipients include the sender and everyone who was a recipient of the initial email.

- **Forward** to create a new email that contains the email message content from the initial email and can be sent to a new recipient, not including the sender of the initial email.

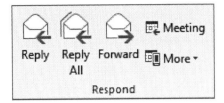

Figure 1-16: The reply options in the Respond command group of the Message tab.

Note: Outlook on the Web

You can access these message response buttons from the drop-down arrow for the **Reply All** command

Inline Replies

In Outlook 2016, you can respond to a message you are viewing in the **Reading** pane using the inline replies feature. When you select any of the message response options within a message that you are viewing in the **Reading** pane, Outlook automatically opens the response form directly in the **Reading** pane, where you can type your response.

If you would rather type your response in a message form rather than using the inline replies option, you can select the **Pop Out** command from the message response in the **Reading** pane to open a separate message window where you can continue to compose your response. You can select **Discard** if you want to abandon the draft email.

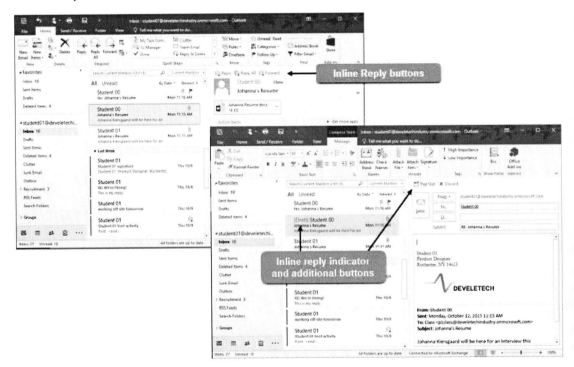

Figure 1-17: Inline replies and the Pop Out command.

Note: Outlook on the Web

Inline replies are the default behavior when composing a response to a selected message. If you want to view the message in a separate window, you can select the **Edit in Separate Window** button that appears in the upper-right corner of the online app window.

Compose Tools Tab

When you use the inline replies option, the **Compose Tools** contextual tab automatically displays. On the tab, the **Message** contextual tab provides access to all the commands that are available on the **Message** tab in a message form.

Additionally, when composing an inline reply, the text *[Draft]* appears in red to the left of the message in the Message list.

ACTIVITY 1-3
Reading and Responding to an Email

Before You Begin
Your instructor has sent you the message with the Subject: We're Hiring!

Scenario
Since you are part of the recruitment team, you have been included on a number of emails regarding the recruitment efforts and potential candidates. The HR recruiter has sent the team an email listing the potential candidates and requesting further candidates, if you know of any. Your friend Adam is a multimedia designer and would be a good candidate for one of the open positions. You need to read and respond to the hiring email with this information. After you reply to the recruiter, you want to forward the email about Develetech's hiring efforts to Adam.

---

1. Read the email with the Subject **We're Hiring!**
   a) In the message list, select the email with the subject line "We're Hiring!"
   b) Read the message body in the **Reading** pane.

2. Reply to all recipients of the message with your response.
   a) On the **Home** tab, select **Respond→Reply All**.

   b) In the message body, type *I have a friend who is a multimedia designer who might be interested. I'll forward this to him.*
      By default, your new message text is blue to indicate that this message is in response to the original message.
   c) Select **Send**.

   > **Note:** Because other students in the class will be using the **Reply All** option, and you were a recipient of the original email, you will receive the responses from your classmates. You will read these responses in Step 4.

3. Forward the We're Hiring! email to your friend Adam.
   a) In the message list, verify that the **We're Hiring!** email is selected.

   b) In the **Reading** pane where the message content is displayed, select **Forward**.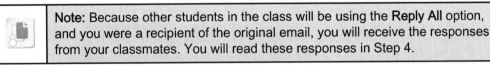
      The **Reading** pane now contains the **To** and **Cc** address fields and a **Send** button. And, the **Subject** has been amended to read **FW: We're Hiring!**
   c) In the **To** field, type the email address of the student one number higher than you
      student##@[your_domain.com]

   > **Note:** If you are the student with the highest number, then send your email to Student00.

   d) In the message body, type *Adam, I thought you might be interested. If so, let me know ASAP.*
      Again, your new message text is blue to reflect that you're forwarding the original message.

   e) Select **Send**.

4. Read one of the replies to the We're Hiring! message that you just received.

   a) In the message list, select one of the responses you've just received from your classmates with the subject line **Re: We're Hiring!**

   b) Observe the message text in the **Reading** pane.

Print Options

Print Options, accessed via the **Backstage** view, allows you to specify the print settings for printing an Outlook item. By default, a preview of your printout appears in the right side of the page. You can change the default printer and the print style (table or memo style) from this **Print** page.

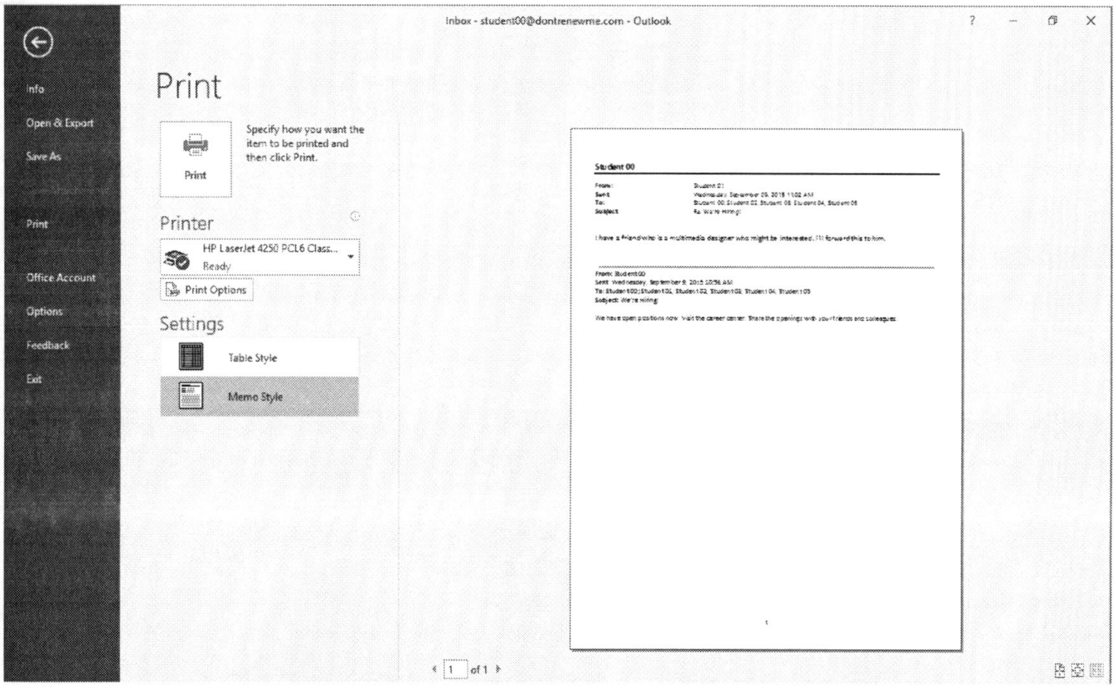

Figure 1-18: Printing from the Backstage view.

You can use the **Print Options** button to open the **Print** dialog box and modify the additional print settings, such as the number of copies being made, the collation setting, the page range, and printing attachments.

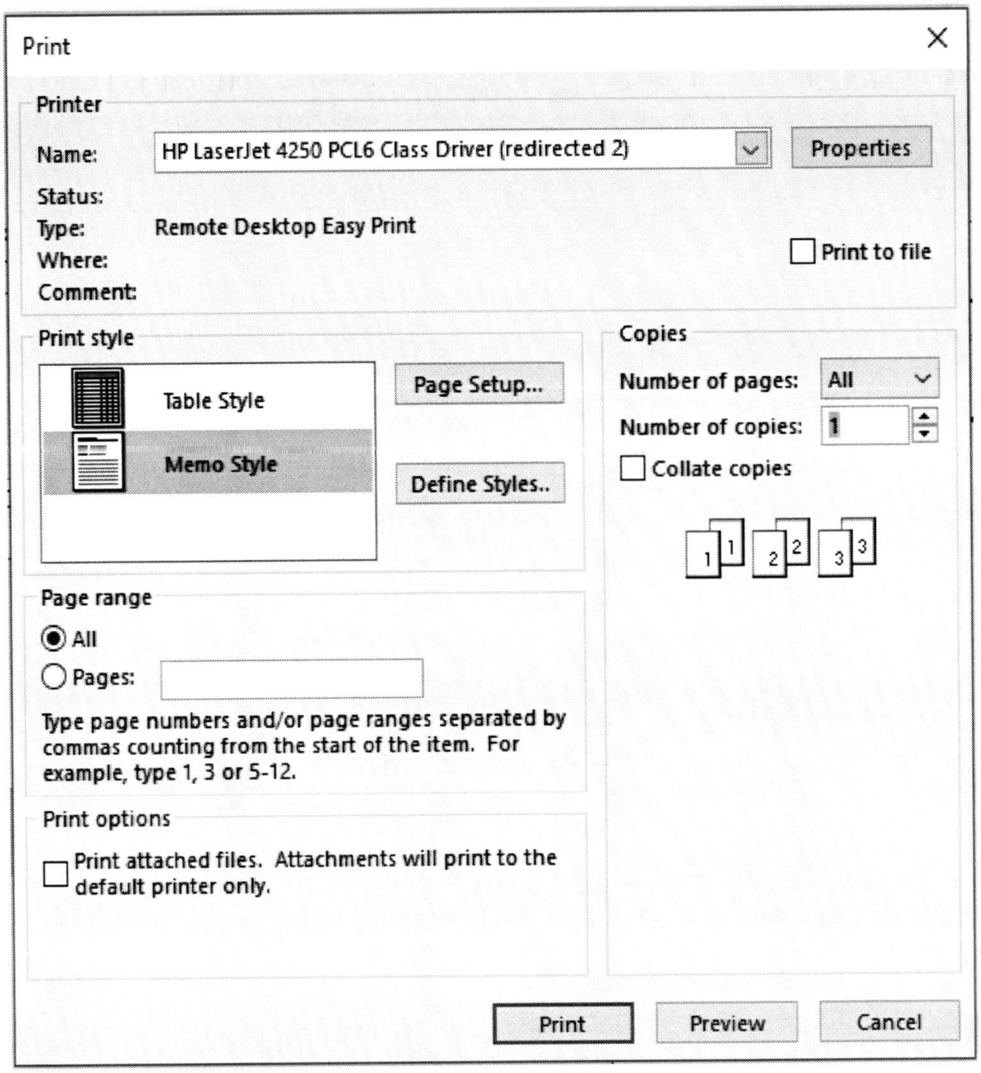

Print ✕

Printer

Name: HP LaserJet 4250 PCL6 Class Driver (redirected 2) ⌄ | Properties

Status:
Type: Remote Desktop Easy Print
Where: ☐ Print to file
Comment:

Print style

Table Style | Page Setup...

Memo Style | Define Styles..

Page range

◉ All
○ Pages:

Type page numbers and/or page ranges separated by
commas counting from the start of the item. For
example, type 1, 3 or 5-12.

Print options

☐ Print attached files. Attachments will print to the
default printer only.

Copies

Number of pages: All ⌄
Number of copies: 1 ⬍
☐ Collate copies

Print | Preview | Cancel

Figure 1-19: The Print dialog box.

Note: Outlook on the Web

When you print in Outlook on the Web, the required steps vary slightly from those used to print in Outlook 2016. You continue to have the ability to preview how the printout will look. From the command bar, select the **More commands** button and then select **Print**. The selected item, such as an email message, is first displayed in a separate window and then the **Print** window containing print settings appears.

ACTIVITY 1-4
Printing an Email Message

Before You Begin

If you do not have a physical printer available in the classroom where you can print documents during activities, a printer driver has been installed on your machine and paused to mimic printing.

Scenario

You want to print out the hiring email. You think that a friend of yours might be interested in applying, and you'd like to pass along this information to her later.

---

1. Preview the printed email from your instructor.
   a) In the message list in the **Content** pane, select any email with the subject line "We're Hiring!"
   b) Select **File** to open the **Backstage** view.
   c) Select **Print**.

   A preview of the email appears in the default Memo Style.

2. Preview and print the email.
   a) Observe the preview in the right side of the window.
   b) Under **Printer**, select the down-arrow on the printer button.
      You can use this button to change the selected printer.
   c) (Optional) Select **Print** if you're attached to a physical printer.

3. Select to return to your Inbox without printing.

> **Note:** If you want to print an email message with default print settings, you do not have to open the message and configure the print settings. You can right-click the email message in the message list and select **Quick Print** from the list of available actions. The email will automatically print to your default printer.

The Deleted Items Folder

You can use one of the following ways to delete a message:

- In the message list, select the message to be deleted and then select **Home→Delete→Delete**.
- In the message list, point to the message to be deleted and select the ✕ button.
- In the message list, drag the message to be deleted from the message list to the **Deleted Items** folder in the **Folder** pane.

Deleted messages and other Outlook items are moved to the **Deleted Items** folder. These items will remain in the **Deleted Items** folder until you manually and permanently delete each item or empty the folder. Items in the **Deleted Items** folder can be recovered to the Inbox or a folder you created until they have been permanently deleted.

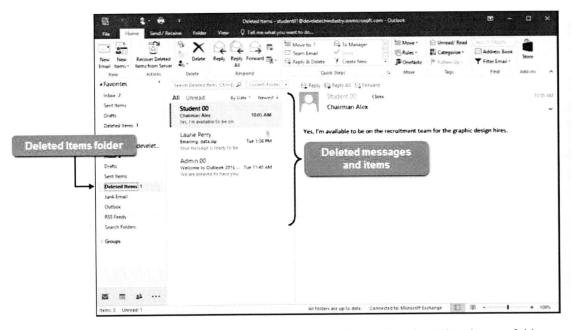

Figure 1–20: Deleted messages and items are moved to and stored in the Deleted Items folder.

> **Access the Checklist tile on your CHOICE Course screen for reference information and job aids on How to Perform Basic Mail Functions.**

ACTIVITY 1-5
Deleting Email Messages

Before You Begin
You have multiple messages that were sent to everyone in the class.

Scenario
You have a couple of old emails that you have read and no longer need to keep in your Inbox. You have the feeling that your **Deleted Items** folder is getting full, so after you delete some of these old messages, you also want to empty the folder to make more available space in your Inbox.

1. Delete unnecessary emails from your Inbox.
    a) In the message list, select any of the messages with the Subject **Chairman Alex**.
    b) Select **Home→Delete→Delete**.

Delete

2. Empty the **Deleted Items** folder.
    a) In the **Folder** pane, select the **Deleted Items** folder.
    b) Verify that the "Chairman Alex" message is in the **Deleted Items** folder.
    c) Right-click the **Deleted Items** folder and select **Empty Folder**.
    d) When prompted to continue, select **Yes**.

> **Note:** If you empty the **Deleted Items** folder prematurely, you can restore the deleted items by selecting the **Deleted Items** folder and then selecting **Home→Actions→Recover Deleted Items from Server**. From the **Recover Deleted Items** dialog box, you can restore any or all of the recently deleted items.

Microsoft OneDrive

Microsoft® OneDrive® provides online file storage, management, and sharing services that you can use to store, share, and collaborate on your Word document files as well as other types of files. There are two versions of OneDrive: personal and business. Anyone can create a personal OneDrive account, but your organization would provide you with the credentials for a business account. With a OneDrive for Business account, you have up to 1 terabyte (TB) of free OneDrive storage. However, if you have a personal Microsoft account (with an @outlook.com email address), the maximum free storage space is 5 GB. You can certainly purchase additional space if you want to.

Managing your files in OneDrive is very similar to managing files in File Explorer. The major difference is that you must upload the files to OneDrive, which enables you to access and work with your files from nearly any location using different devices. From within the OneDrive browser window, select **Upload→Files** or **Upload→Folder** and then navigate to the file or folder you want to upload. While working in a particular Office 2016 application, another way to "upload" a file to OneDrive is to select **File→Save As** and then select **OneDrive** to be the **Save As** location.

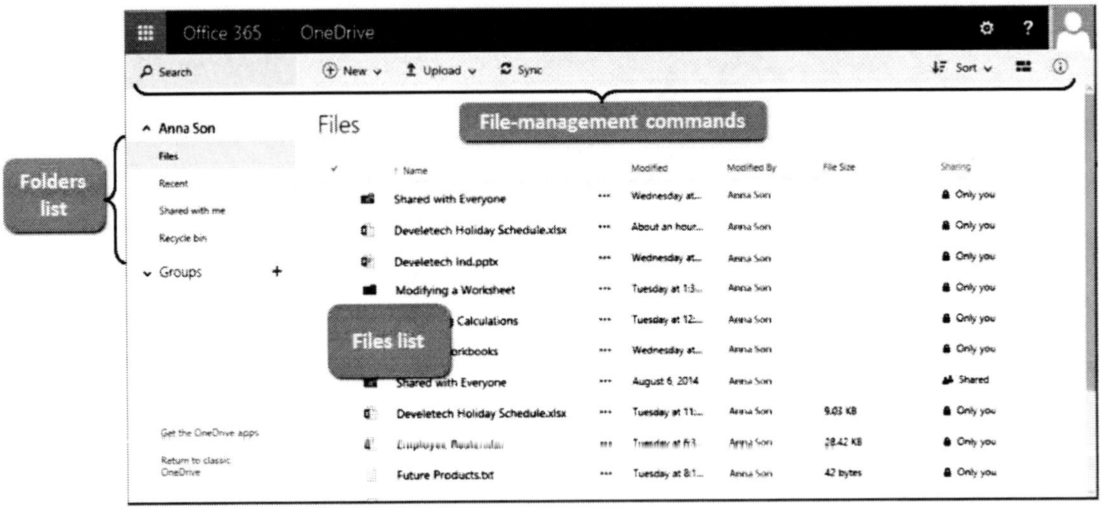

Figure 1-21: A sample OneDrive for Business page.

ACTIVITY 1-6

Signing in to Office 365 and OneDrive (Optional Instructor Demo)

Data File

C:\091058Data\Getting Started with Outlook 2016\logo.png

Before You Begin

You have an Office 365 login user name and password.

Scenario

Develetech now uses the Office 2016 applications through their cloud-based Office 365 subscription. While you are becoming comfortable working in the desktop versions of Office, the features of the Office 365 apps are new and unfamiliar. You're especially interested in the collaboration and mobility capabilities of these online apps. After signing in to Office 365, you'll check out the file storage app called OneDrive.

---

1. From the Windows **Start** screen, open Microsoft Edge and go to the Office 365 login screen and sign in to Office 365.

   a) Select the **Microsoft Edge** tile. ▨

   b) In the **Address** box at the top of the screen, enter *https://login.microsoftonline.com*

2. Enter your credentials to sign in.

   a) In the **User ID** box, enter your user ID, including the @ symbol and the domain name.

   b) In the **Password** box, enter your password.

   c) Select **Sign in**.
   When Office 365 opens, your Outlook mail is displayed.

3. Open OneDrive.

   a) Observe the header at the top of the Outlook window.

   ⊞ Office 365 │ Outlook   ♠ ✿ ?

   When you sign in to your Office 365 account, your Outlook mail is opened first.

   b) In the upper-left corner of the window, select the **App Launcher** icon. ⊞

   c) From the menu, select the **OneDrive** tile.

d) Observe the elements of the OneDrive user interface.

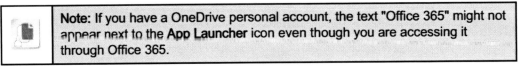

The Office 365 header at the top of the screen displays both the App Launcher and OneDrive to indicate that you are working in the online apps. At the right end of the header bar, there are buttons to access **Notifications**, **Settings**, **Help**, and your account settings, from left to right respectively. Immediately below the Office 365 header are context-specific commands. In OneDrive, these commands are used to perform basic file management tasks, such as creating new Office files as well as uploading, syncing, sorting, and viewing files.

> **Note:** If you have a OneDrive personal account, the text "Office 365" might not appear next to the **App Launcher** icon even though you are accessing it through Office 365.

4. From the student data files, upload the Develetech logo to OneDrive.
   a) From the command bar, select **Upload→Files**.
   b) In the **Open** dialog box, navigate to the **C:\091058Data\Getting Started with Outlook 2016** folder.
   c) Select the **logo.png** image file, and then select **Open**.
   d) Observe the **Files** list.
   The uploaded Develetech logo image now appears in the **Files** list.

> **Note:** You can select **Upload→Folder** to upload multiple files in an entire folder at one time. According to Microsoft, you can use the drag-and-drop method to upload files but only if you're using Microsoft® Internet Explorer® 11.

   e) Select the check mark column to the left of the file name, as indicated.

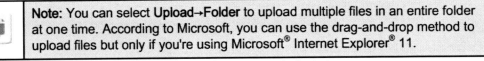

   f) Observe the file management commands.

When a file is selected, file management commands become available. You can use these commands to delete, move, share, or otherwise manage your OneDrive files. You can access additional commands by selecting the **More commands** button. If the file was associated with an app, such as a Word document, then an **Open** command would be available. From this command, you would have the option to open the file in either the online or desktop application.

Outlook on the Web

As part of the Office set of apps, Outlook is included in your Office 365 subscription. You can access this scaled-down version of Outlook through your web browser with an Internet connection. You can use Outlook to read and respond to email, organize your messages, and participate in online groups. The type of Office 365 subscription you have—**Business** or **Personal**—will dictate Outlook's appearance and the available features.

- When you sign in to your Office 365 for Business account, you are automatically directed to your Inbox. You will immediately notice that the web-version of Outlook is a simplified version of the Outlook desktop application. However, many of the familiar mail features are available and function the same. You can use the **App Launcher** icon to access tiles for the other Outlook items, such as the **Calendar**, **People**, and **Tasks**.

- You can also access Outlook on the web with a personal Outlook account by signing in with an email address that ends with @outlook.com, @live.com, @hotmail.com, or @msn.com. As expected, your Inbox opens and looks similar to the Outlook for Business interface with a slightly different set of commands. If you are using a free Microsoft account, such as the one shown in the following figure, an advertising pane will appear along the right side of the window.

Figure 1-22: The Outlook for Business and the personal Outlook on the web user interfaces.

Some of the major differences between using Outlook 2016 desktop application and Outlook on the web are:

- You must use the **App Launcher** icon ▦ to navigate to your **Calendar**, **People**, and **Tasks** by selecting the applicable tile.
- Instead of the familiar Office ribbon, commands are located on the task bar as indicated in the previous figure. In online Help, this might also be referred to as the command bar.
- The **Notes** feature is not available from within Outlook; however, you can use the OneNote® Online app that is included in the Office 365 suite of apps.
- The **Clutter** feature is available in both applications, but you must activate it from within Outlook on the web.

ACTIVITY 1-7

Navigating in Outlook on the Web (Optional Instructor Demo)

Before You Begin

You are signed in to Office 365, and Outlook on the web is open.

Scenario

Before you can take full advantage of the collaboration features, you need to familiarize yourself with the Outlook on the web user interface.

1. Open the **Outlook** web app.

   a) In the upper-left corner of the window, select the **App Launcher** icon. ⊞

   b) From the menu, select the **Mail** tile.

   In the web browser, Outlook is quite similar as the desktop application. The window is divided into three panes—**Folder**, **Message List**, and **Reading** pane. At the right end of the Outlook header bar are buttons to access **Notifications**, **Settings**, **Help**, and your account settings, from left to right, respectively. Instead of the familiar Office ribbon, immediately below the Office 365 header are context-specific commands. In Outlook, these commands are used to perform basic mail tasks, such as creating a new message, replying to a message, and archiving a message to name a few.

   c) Observe the **Folders** pane.
   Located along the left side of the window, you can expand and collapse the Inbox folders as you like. You can also access your Outlook groups from this pane as well.

   d) Under **Folders**, select **More** to view additional folders.
   You can now see the complete list of your Outlook folders, including the **Favorites**.

   > **Note:** If you are using a personal Outlook account, the complete list of folders is automatically displayed.

2. Read the messages in the Inbox.

   a) Select any Inbox message.

   b) Observe the command bar.

   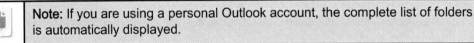

   When you select a message, the task bar reflects the available actions that you can take.

   c) Read the message text in the **Reading** pane.
   The position of the **Reading** pane can be changed to display across the bottom of the window or hide it completely.

3. Create and send a message to everyone in the class.

   a) In the task bar, select **New**.
   A new message form is displayed in the **Reading** pane. Similar to using the **Pop Out** command, you can select the **Edit in Separate Window** button to open the message form in a new browser window.

   b) In the **To** address field, enter *Class* to send the message to everyone.

   c) In the **Subject** field, enter *Demo Message*

   d) In the message body, type *This message is being composed and sent from Outlook on the web.*

   e) Select the **Send** button.

   f) Ask one of the students to select **Reply all→Reply** to the demo message that they received.

   > **Note:** If you select the **Reply all** button, everyone in the address fields will receive your reply. You must intentionally select **Reply** from the drop-down menu to reply to only the sender.

4. Print a selected message.

   a) Select any email message.

   b) In the task bar, select the **More Commands** button. [•••]

   c) From the list of commands, select **Print**.
   The selected message is first displayed in a separate browser window and then the **Print** window opens. You can preview the printout and modify the print settings, as desired.

   d) Select **Cancel** to close the Print window.

   e) Close the message window.

5. Use the **App Launcher** to view your calendar, contacts, and tasks.

   a) Select the **App Launcher** icon and then select the **Calendar** tile.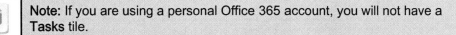
   Rather than selecting an icon from the **Navigation bar**, you access your calendar from the App Launcher. In the Office 365 for Business account, your calendar opens within the same Outlook on the Web window. However, if you are using a personal account, the calendar opens on a new browser tab. The available commands have been reduced to adding new calendar events, sharing, and printing. You can use the commands in the upper-right area of the window to change the calendar view, if desired.

   b) Select the **App Launcher** icon and then select the **People** tile.
   With the exception of the Outlook ribbon, this app containing your personal contacts looks and acts similar to your **Contacts** view in Outlook 2016.

   c) Select the **App Launcher** icon and then select the **Tasks** tile.
   Again, like the **Tasks** view in the desktop application, your tasks are created and managed in the same way.

   > **Note:** If you are using a personal Office 365 account, you will not have a **Tasks** tile.

   d) From the **App Launcher**, select the **Mail** tile.

6. Observe your **Mail** app settings.

   a) At the right end of the Office 365 header, select the **Settings** icon.
   Instead of **File** tab and a **Backstage** view, you can use the **Settings** icon to access the Outlook options.

b) Scroll to the bottom of the **Settings** pane and observe the **My app settings** section.

> **My app settings**
>
> Office 365
>
> Mail
>
> Calendar
>
> People
>
> Yammer

c) Select **Mail**.
Using this link, you can access numerous options to control the automatic processing, account information, and layout settings for your Outlook mail. This is similar to using the **Backstage** view in the desktop application.

7. Access online Help.

   a) Select the **Help** icon. **?**
   b) In the **Tell Me** box, enter *keyboard shortcuts*
   The **Help** pane displays a list of links to suggested help pages.
   c) Select one of the suggested links.
   The help page opens in a new browser tab.

8. Return to Outlook 2016 to verify that messages exchanged in Outlook on the Web are reflected in the desktop application.

   a) Verify that your Outlook on the Web Inbox contains the reply sent from the student.
   b) Close the web browser and all open tabs.
   c) Switch to Outlook 2016 and point out that the reply sent from the student also appears in the desktop application.

TOPIC C

Access Outlook Help

Knowing the basics for navigating the Outlook interface and performing some email functions is important to get you started. But what if you forget how to perform an action or want to do something more advanced? Knowing how to access and search **Outlook Help** to find the information you are looking for will help you be more productive when using email to communicate.

Tell Me Feature

Have you ever spent too much time looking through the ribbon to find a specific action you need to take in one of the Office apps? *Tell Me* is a new feature designed to help save you time by finding the specific action you need to perform for you, with just a few keystrokes. The **Tell Me** box is at the top-right corner of the ribbon. Just start typing in a few keywords for the action you are looking for and the "word-wheeling" functionality will automatically try to contextually determine what you are searching for and provide a few possible results. Then, choose the function you are looking for from the list of results, and Tell Me will perform the action for you.

For example, say that you want to address changes that have been made to a document you are working on in Microsoft® Word but can't remember where to find that action on the ribbon. If you type "change" in the **Tell Me** box, Tell Me provides you with the option to go to the next change, go to the previous change, accept or reject changes, toggle track changes, find out more contextual information about making changes using Smart Lookup, or accessing the Office Help topic about making changes.

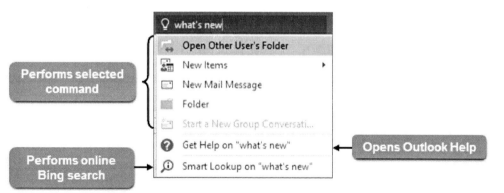

Figure 1-23: The Tell Me feature.

Whenever you select the **Tell Me** box, a list of the most commonly searched-for actions for the application or the last five actions you searched for will appear, saving you even more time.

> **Note: Outlook on the Web**
>
> You can access the **Tell Me** feature and online Help documents by selecting the **Help** icon **?** at the right end of the Office 365 header—immediately to the left of your account profile icon. In the **Help** pane, you can enter a word or phrase in the **Tell Me** box, select one of the suggested help links, or select **Help** at the bottom of the pane to open Outlook on the Web help. Once open, the online app Help window works the same as the desktop application Help window.

Outlook Help

Outlook Help is a repository of information regarding the features and functionalities available in Outlook. **Outlook Help** can be accessed when you are online. You can use one of the following methods to access help:

- Enter a word or question in the **Tell Me** box and then select the **Get Help** option.

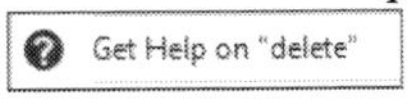

  ❓ Get Help on "delete"

- Select **File** and then select the  [?] button.
- Press **F1**.

When launched, the **Outlook Help** window displays links to the top categories of topics about working with Outlook. You can also use the **Instant Search** box to enter a keyword and perform a keyword specific search.

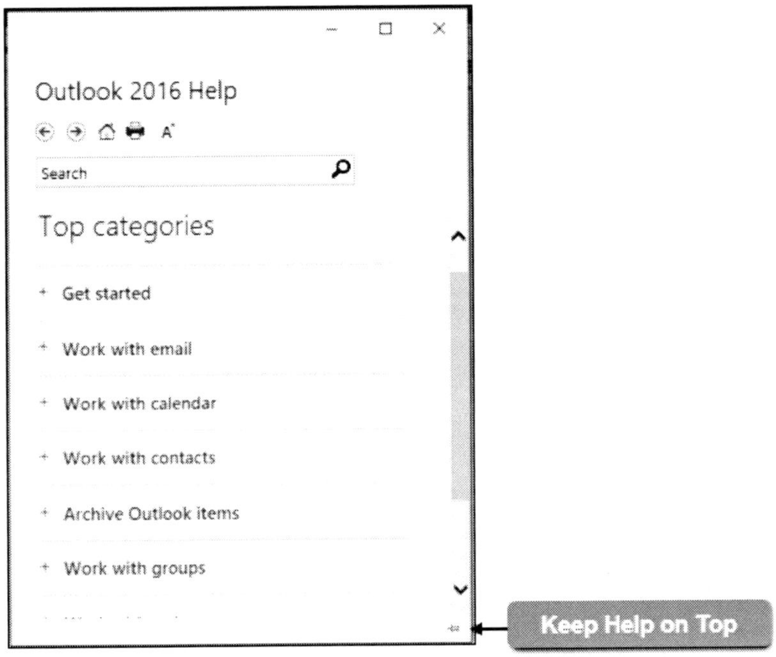

Figure 1-24: The Outlook Help window.

Outlook Help Toolbar Buttons

In the **Outlook Help** window, there are a number of toolbar buttons that help you navigate through **Help** or select other options available to you.

Toolbar Button	Description
Back	Navigates back to the previous page.
Forward	Navigates forward to the next page. This button is only accessible once you have used the **Back** button to visit the previous page; then you can navigate forward to a page you already visited.
Home	Returns to the home screen of the **Outlook Help** tool.
Print	Prints the page you are currently viewing.
Use Large Text	Makes the text on screen larger than the default size to make it easier to read. Select the button again to return the text to the smaller, default font size.

Toolbar Button	Description
Keep Help On Top	Keeps the **Help** window on top of other Outlook windows that you have opened. The default setting when you launch **Help** is **Keep on Top**. If you do not want the **Outlook Help** window to display on top of other open Outlook windows, select the button; the button will now be activated and will display as **Not on Top**.

Access the Checklist tile on your CHOICE Course screen for reference information and job aids on How to Access Outlook Help.

ACTIVITY 1-8
Using the Tell Me Feature

Scenario

Since you are new to using Outlook as your email application, there may be some things about it that you aren't comfortable using or need some help with. You want to explore the **Outlook Help** and Tell Me features so you can easily access help when you need it.

1. Use **Tell Me** to search for information about mail.
   a) In the **Tell Me** box, type *mail*

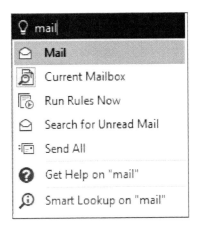

   As you begin to type, the Tell Me feature offers suggestions that might be of interest to you based on the keywords. Selecting a suggestion will automatically perform the command unless the suggested option contains a solid arrow indicating additional options. At the bottom of the list are links to **Help** and **Smart Lookup**.
   b) Select **Get Help on "mail"**
   Outlook 2016 Help opens in a separate window with "mail' in the **Search** bar and a list of available help articles.

2. Search for information using the **Help** window.
   a) From the list of help articles, select one that interests you.
   You can select links within an article to dig deeper into a subject.
   b) Use the toolbar buttons to navigate back and forward among the open help articles to return to the homepage.

   ⊖ ⊕ ⌂ 🖨 A˙

3. Search for information using the **Instant Search** box and a keyword.
   a) Select the **Instant Search** box, type a keyword or phrase of your choice, and press **Enter** or select the **Search** button. 🔎
   b) From the search result list, select an article and review the information.
   c) Close the **Outlook Help** window.

Summary

In this lesson, you became familiar with the Outlook 2016 interface and performed basic email functions that included creating, reading, and responding to email messages. You also explored the variety of ways to access help when you need it. Knowing your way around the interface and how to complete these basic emailing tasks will allow you to begin working in Outlook immediately.

Which component of the Outlook interface do you think will be most important or useful to you in your everyday life? Why?

What is your own personal experience with using email and a corporate email client like Outlook in a professional setting? Did using email make communicating with your coworkers easier or more difficult?

Note: Check your CHOICE Course screen for opportunities to interact with your classmates, peers, and the larger CHOICE online community about the topics covered in this course or other topics you are interested in. From the Course screen you can also access available resources for a more continuous learning experience.

2 | Formatting Messages

Lesson Time: 45 minutes

Lesson Objectives

In this lesson, you will:

- Use the address book to add recipients.

- Check spelling and grammar.

- Apply formatting to message content.

Lesson Introduction

Once you are familiar with the Microsoft® Office Outlook® 2016 interface and how to use its basic email functions, you are ready to start using Outlook to its fullest capabilities. Making sure that your messages are free of spelling and grammatical errors, as well as applying some basic formatting, enables you to feel confident that you are sending professional looking messages. In this lesson, you will compose and format messages.

TOPIC A

Add Message Recipients

Without having someone to send your messages to, the concept of email is pretty much useless. When composing an email, one of your first steps is determining who you want to send a message to and then addressing the message to those recipients. Outlook provides features that can help you quickly and easily select your recipients from a single location, making addressing an email a more streamlined process.

The Address Book

An *address book* in Outlook is a repository for your contacts. Your contacts can include those you have created and saved in Outlook, those you have imported into Outlook from another email client, or those created by your organization. You can use the address book when composing a new message to find and select those contacts to whom you want to send the email message. When you begin typing a recipient's name in the **To**, **Cc**, or **Bcc** field, Outlook's AutoComplete feature attempts to guess your intended recipient by displaying address book contacts that match what you're typing. If you have more than one contact in your address book that matches what you're typing, you can use **Ctrl+K** to open the **Check Names** dialog box and manually select the contact from a list.

 Note: You can have more than one address book in Outlook to help you organize your contacts for easy access.

Microsoft Exchange Server

Microsoft Exchange Server is a mail server application that manages the email messages and other types of communications, such as meeting invitations, that are sent through Outlook between users on a network. Microsoft® Exchange Server acts as the communication platform through which all these communications are filtered.

 Note: Microsoft Exchange Server is not required for Outlook to manage communications; Outlook can also manage Internet email methods like Post Office Protocol version 3 (POP3) and Internet Message Access Protocol (IMAP). If you are using Office 2016 through an Office 365 subscription, then Microsoft is managing the Exchange server.

Global Address List

The *Global Address List* is a list of all users, shared resources, and distribution groups that have been created and networked on the Microsoft Exchange Server for an organization. Global Address Lists are created and maintained by the Exchange administrator. Only users with an email account on the Exchange Server can access a Global Address List.

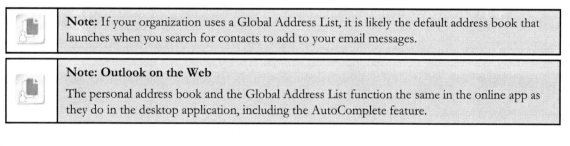

Figure 2-1: A Global Address List in the address book.

> **Note:** If your organization uses a Global Address List, it is likely the default address book that launches when you search for contacts to add to your email messages.

> **Note: Outlook on the Web**
>
> The personal address book and the Global Address List function the same in the online app as they do in the desktop application, including the AutoComplete feature.

MailTips

MailTips is a feature provided when Outlook 2016 is configured with Microsoft Exchange Server or with Exchange Online. MailTips provide real-time feedback about the message you are creating. While you're composing your message, Outlook and Exchange work together to determine if there are any issues that might prevent your message from being sent or delivered successfully. For example, a large recipient group or an external recipient might prevent the successful delivery of your message. If any issues or important points for notification are detected, the MailTip is displayed between the ribbon and the address fields in your message.

MailTips can be turned on or off, and can be configured to only display notifications for certain issues. From the **Backstage** view, select **Options→Mail→MailTip Options** to modify the settings.

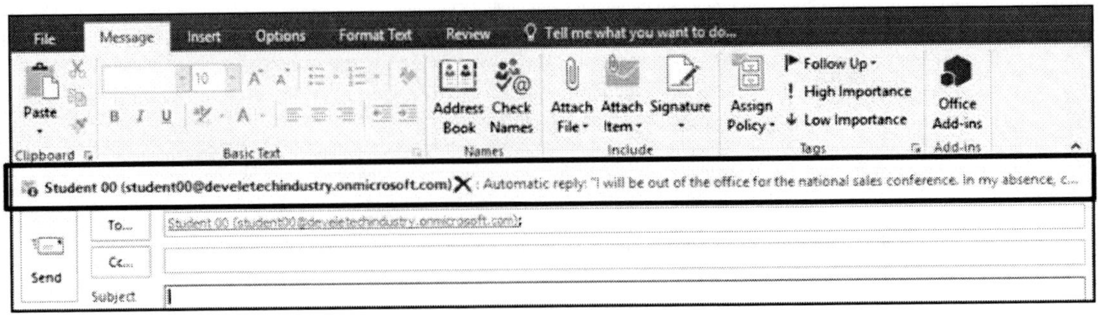

Figure 2-2: A MailTip displaying the recipient's automatic out of office reply.

Aooooo the Checklist tile on your CHOICE Course screen for reference information and job aids on **How to Add Recipients to an Email Message.**

ACTIVITY 2-1
Using the Address Book when Composing a New Message

Data File

C:\091058Data\Formatting Messages\greg.txt

Scenario

You've been asked to be one of the lead points of contact for the recruiting efforts at Develetech. Part of your responsibilities will be sending pre-screening emails to the recruitment team containing information about each candidate that has applied. You want these emails to be polished and professional because many people throughout the company will be included on these emails. The first email you will send to the team is about Greg Shannon.

1. Create a new email message.
   a) On the **Home** tab, in the **New** command group, select **New Mail**.

   [New Email icon]

2. Select the odd numbered class members as your primary recipients by using the Global Address List to add them to the **To** field.

   a) Select [To...] to open the **Select Names** dialog box.

   > [icon] **Note:** The dialog box automatically defaults to a name only search within the Global Address List as the address book. Verify that these options are chosen.

   b) In the list of names, select **Student 01**, press and hold **Ctrl**, and continue to select the remaining odd-numbered email addresses.
   c) Select the **To** button.

   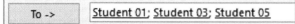

   This action entered the selected email addresses in the **To** field at the bottom of the **Select Names** dialog box.

3. Add the even-numbered students to the **Cc** field.
   a) In the **Select Names** dialog box, select **Student 02**, press and hold **Ctrl**, and continue to select the remaining even-numbered students.

b) Select the 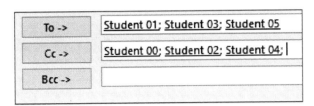 button.

To ->	Student 01; Student 03; Student 05
Cc ->	Student 00; Student 02; Student 04;
Bcc ->	

c) Select **OK**.

4. Enter **Greg Shannon info** as the **Subject** of the email message.
   a) Select the **Subject** field, and type *[your initials] Greg Shannon info*
   b) Select the message body and notice that the title bar of the message changes to "Greg Shannon info - Message (HTML)."

5. From the data file **greg.txt**, copy and paste the message content that includes typographical errors.
   a) In the Windows taskbar, open File Explorer and navigate to the course data files.
   b) Open **C:\091058Data\Formatting Messages\greg.txt** and select all of the text by pressing **Ctrl+A**.
   c) Press **Ctrl+C** to copy the selected text.
   d) Use the Windows taskbar to select the unfinished email message.
   e) In the message body, press **Ctrl+V** to paste the selected text.

   Greg has a lot of experience in mnay related fields. His resune is attached for your review. Let me know by tomorrow if you think its worth having Greg come in for an interview.

 Note: If you choose to type the text, be sure to include the typographical errors. These errors will be fixed when you check for spelling and grammar.

   f) Leave the Greg Shannon info message open for the next activity.

6. Close Notepad without saving changes to greg.txt.

TOPIC B

Check Spelling and Grammar

You have added text into your message and have formatted the message content to your liking. Before sending any message, it is a good idea to make sure that your message is free of any egregious errors. In this topic, you will check spelling and grammar in your message.

You're only human, and humans make mistakes. Whether entering a quick message to a friend or composing a complex email to a coworker or boss, it is highly likely that you will make some mistakes in your spelling or grammar usage within your message content. Sending a message with errors can detract from the message you are trying to convey and, worse, make you look unprofessional. Using the spelling and grammar tools provided in Outlook 2016 helps prevent unwanted and potentially embarrassing errors in your email messages.

The AutoCorrect Feature

The *AutoCorrect* feature is a tool in Outlook that checks for common typing errors, including spelling and grammar errors, capitalization mistakes, and other typographical mistakes. By default, spelling and grammar are automatically checked as you type your message. If you make a mistake while typing and AutoCorrect can determine what was intended, it will automatically correct the error. For more complicated mistakes that AutoCorrect cannot fix automatically, it will notify you visually in the message that there is an error using wavy underlines of various colors; wavy red underlines indicate a possible spelling error, wavy blue underlines indicate a possible word choice error, and wavy green underlines indicate a possible grammatical error.

When AutoCorrect notifies you that there is a possible error, you can right-click the word or words with the error, and AutoCorrect provides a list of possible corrections. Within this list, you can also choose to ignore the correction, add the word to your AutoCorrect dictionary, or configure AutoCorrect options.

	To...	Student 01; Student 03; Student 05
Send	Cc...	Student 00; Student 02; Student 04
	Subject	Greg Shannon info

Greg has a lot of experience in mnay related fields. His resune is attached for your review. Let me know by tomorrow if you think its worth having Greg come in for an interview.

Figure 2-3: The wavy colored underlines indicate errors detected by AutoCorrect.

> **Note: Outlook on the Web**
>
> In the online app, there is no **Spelling and Grammar** dialog box or a command to access it; however, the **AutoCorrect** feature will indicate incorrect words with red, wavy underlines.

The Spelling and Grammar Checker

Outlook comes with a Spelling and Grammar checker that you can use to detect spelling and grammatical errors in your email message before you send it. When you have completed composing your message, you can run the Spelling and Grammar checker, which is located on the **Review** tab of the ribbon. If any spelling or grammar errors in your email message are detected during the Spelling and Grammar check, the **Spelling and Grammar** dialog box will display. For each of the errors detected, the **Spelling and Grammar** dialog box provides a suggestion for how to correct the error. When no more errors exist, or you have addressed all the detected errors in the email, Outlook displays a message that the spelling and grammar check is complete.

Components of the Spelling and Grammar Dialog Box

The **Spelling and Grammar** dialog box has a number of components and accompanying actions to use to correct mistakes in your email messages.

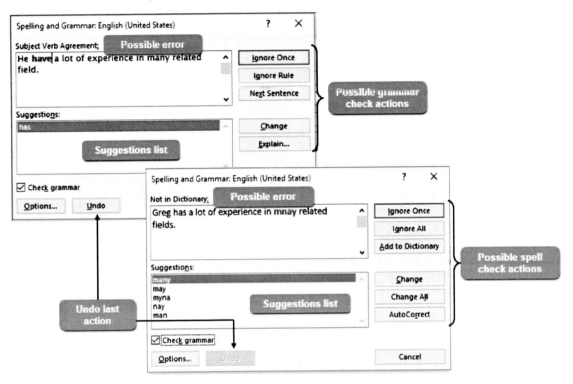

Figure 2-4: The components and options in the Spelling and Grammar dialog box.

Dialog Box Component	Description
Possible error	The top section of the dialog box displays the possible error that the Spelling and Grammar Checker has identified, which may include any words that you have misspelled, possible word choice errors, or grammatical errors.
	Note: The title above this section will reflect the type of error being identified. For example, "Not in Dictionary" is used for misspelled words. Grammar errors might be more specifically identified, such "Subject Verb Agreement."
Suggestions	This section offers possible words that you intended to type, the correct spelling of a misspelled word, or the correct grammar usage for a grammatical error.

Dialog Box Component	Description
Possible spell check actions	For the word that has been detected as misspelled and is displayed in the **Not in Dictionary** section, there are a number of actions you can choose to take based on the error and suggestion: • **Ignore Once:** Ignores the spelling error. It will advance you to the next error, if there are any further errors. • **Ignore All:** Ignores all instances of spelling errors that were detected, and ends the spelling and grammar check. • **Add to Dictionary:** If the word that has been detected as an error is actually correct (such a term commonly used in your specific business), you can add the word to your dictionary. It will not change the word in your current message, and will not detect it as an error in future spelling and grammar checks. • **Change:** Changes the spelling of the word to the option from the **Suggestions** list that you have chosen. • **Change All:** Changes all instances of spelling errors that were detected to an option from the **Suggestions** list. • **AutoCorrect:** Will apply the AutoCorrect option. If there is a word that you know you often misspell, you can use AutoCorrect to correct the word in this instance to the suggested change, and Outlook will save the suggested option and automatically change it to that option every time you misspell the word.
Possible grammar check actions	For the phrase that has been detected as grammatically incorrect and is displayed in the **Not in Dictionary** section, there are a number of actions you can choose to take based on the error and suggestion: • **Ignore Once:** Ignores the grammar error and the suggested change. It will advance you to the next error, if there are any further errors. If you run the Spelling and Grammar Checker again, this error will be detected again. • **Ignore Rule:** Ignores the error and the suggested change, and ignores the rule for that error. It will advance you to the next error, if there are any further errors. If you run the Spelling and Grammar Checker again, this error will not be detected again. • **Next Sentence:** Advances to the next sentence without applying any changes to the message. It will advance you to the next error, if there are any further errors. If you run the Spelling and Grammar Checker again, this error will be detected again. • **Change:** Changes the grammatically incorrect phrase to the correct option from the **Suggestions** list that you have chosen. • **Explain:** If you are not sure why the phrase is grammatically incorrect, Explain will tell you which grammar or usage rule has been violated.
Options	The **Options** button opens the **Editor Options** dialog box, where you can specify settings and options for how spelling and grammatical errors are handled.
Undo	The **Undo** button undoes the last action that you performed in the Spelling and Grammar check.
Close or Cancel	The **Close** or **Cancel** button cancels the Spelling and Grammar check, and closes the dialog box. Depending on the actions you have previously taken within the dialog box, this button will change to reflect an appropriate action that can be taken, **Close** or **Cancel**.

Note: When you use **Change** or **Change All**, unless you select an option in the **Suggestions** list directly, it will replace the error with the first suggestion in the list. Before selecting this option, verify that this suggested change is really what you want.

Access the Checklist tile on your CHOICE Course screen for reference information and job aids on How to Check Spelling and Grammar.

ACTIVITY 2-2
Checking Spelling and Grammar in a Message

Scenario

Now that you have composed the text in your email about Greg Shannon to share with the other members of the recruitment team, you want to check the content for any spelling or grammar errors. You don't want to send the email to your teammates with any mistakes, which would make you look unprofessional. You will use the Spelling and Grammar Checker in Outlook to double-check your email message.

1. Run the Spelling and Grammar Checker on your message content.

    a) In the **Greg Shannon info** message, place your insertion point at the beginning of the message content.

    b) On the ribbon, select the **Review** tab, and then select **Spelling & Grammar**. (Or, press **F7**.)

Not in Dictionary:	
Greg has a lot of experience in **mnay** related fields.	Ignore Once
	Ignore All
	Add to Dictionary
Suggestions:	
many	Change
may	
myna	Change All
nay	
man	AutoCorrect

    The **Spelling and Grammar** dialog box opens with the first error highlighted.

2. Correct the errors detected in the Spelling and Grammar check.

    a) In the **Spelling and Grammar** dialog box, in the **Not in Dictionary** section, verify that "mnay" is highlighted in red, indicating a misspelling.

    b) In the **Suggestions** list, verify that **many** is selected, and select **Change**.
    This corrects the spelling of "many" and moves to the next error.

    c) Correct the spelling of the word "resune" by changing it to **résumé**.

    d) Fix the possible word choice error of "its" by changing it to **it's**.
    When all errors have been addressed, the "Spelling and grammar check is complete" message appears.

    e) Select **OK** to close the "Spell check complete" message.

TOPIC C

Format Message Content

When you create and send a basic email, you might just find yourself typing your message content into the message body. But, what if you have text you want to paste into your message from another document, that perhaps has different formatting? In this topic, you will format message content.

When you send a basic email message, you might not be too concerned about how your message content is formatted. But as you begin to work with more complex message content, especially in a business setting, you may find you need to format your message content for consistency or professional appearance. Outlook provides a number of tools to help you format your message content to help you create polished, professional-looking emails.

Message Formats

The default message format in Outlook is HTML. If you are concerned that any of your recipients cannot receive messages in HTML format, you can choose to send your messages to them in a different message format to ensure that they can receive and read your email message. You can change the message format for one specific message, change the message format for messages sent to specific users who may not support a certain message format, or you can change the message format for all messages you send.

The following message formats are available in Outlook:

- **Hyper Text Markup Language** (HTML)—which is the primary language used to write web content.
- **Rich Text Format** (RTF)—which is a Microsoft-specific format.
- **Plain Text**

HTML and RTF messages can be formatted with traditional document options, such as fonts, colors, bullet lists, and images. Plain text messages cannot be formatted with any of these text formatting options.

 Note: Not all email clients support all of these formats; while most email applications support HTML, plain text is the only format that is supported by all applications. RTF is only supported by Microsoft email clients.

 Note: Outlook on the Web

When composing a new message, you can select the **More commands** button to switch between HTML and plain text formats.

Paste Options

Outlook 2016, like many other Microsoft Office applications, provides a number of paste options that you can use when copying and pasting text or objects from another location into your message content.

The paste options can be accessed either by right-clicking the message body to open the contextual menu or by clicking the **Paste** command in the **Clipboard** command group, on either the **Message** or **Format Text** tabs on the ribbon.

 Note: You must copy the content you want to paste into your message before selecting your paste options. Depending on the content you have copied, different paste options will be available to use.

Paste Option	Description
	Keep Source Formatting: the content, when pasted into the message body, retains the formatting from the original source content.
	Merge Formatting: the content, when pasted into the message body, adapts the formatting of the location or document where it has been pasted.
	Keep Text Only: the content, when pasted into the message body, is pasted without any formatting or graphics at all, and is simply pasted as plain text.
	Use Destination Theme: if content has been copied from a source that has been formatted with styles or themes, the content retains the style name that was applied to the text in the original source, but uses the style definition of the message where the text was pasted.

> **Note: Outlook on the Web**
>
> In the online app, the available paste options are **Paste as is**, **Paste simple HTML**, and **Paste text** .

Paste Special

The **Paste Special** command lets you select a more specific format for content that you are pasting into your message body. **Paste Special** can only be accessed by selecting the **Paste** command in the **Clipboard** command group on either the **Message** or **Format Text** tabs on the ribbon. When you select this paste option, the **Paste Special** dialog box appears, where you can select the desired format for your text. The formats available depend on the content that has been copied, and what formats the application supports where it is being pasted.

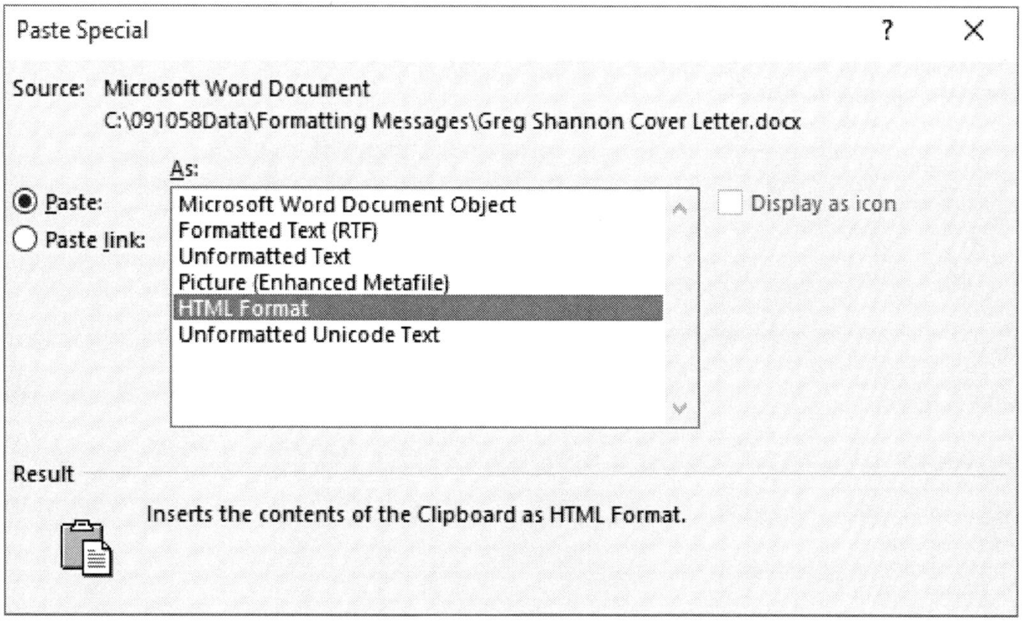

Figure 2-5: The Paste Special option lets you select from a variety of supported formats.

Live Preview

Live Preview is a feature in Outlook 2016 and other Office 2016 products that provides a sneak peek of what formatting changes will look like before they're applied. Often, you will find it helpful to change the formatting of your message content. First, select the text you want to format, and then hover over the desired formatting options (such as text color) to see how the text will look before you actually apply the formatting.

 Note: Live Preview applies to a number of formatting options in Outlook that are related to Styles and Themes. Styles and Themes are covered in more detail later.

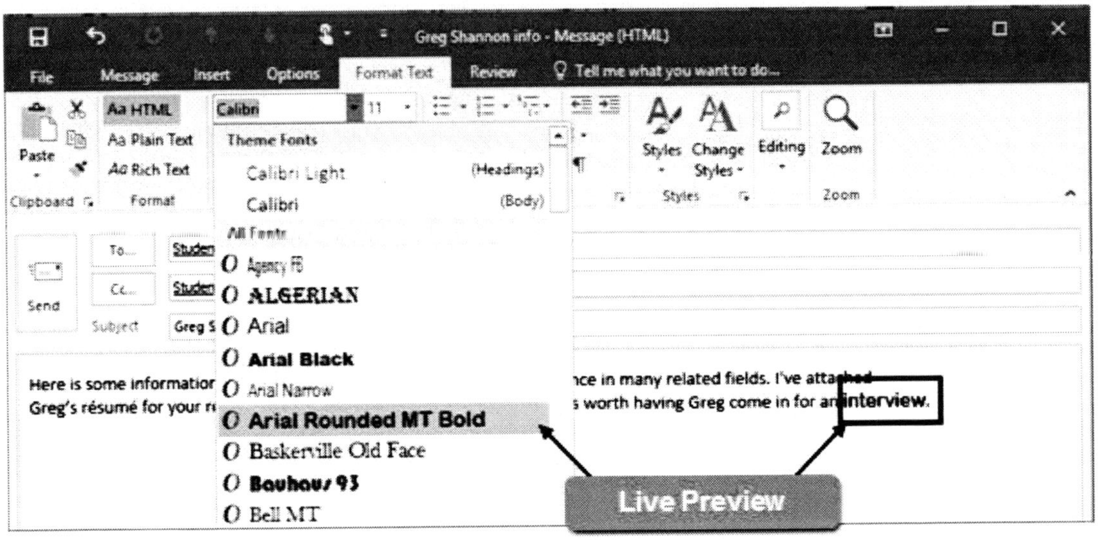

Figure 2-6: Live Preview displays the results of applying a different font to selected message content.

 Note: Outlook on the Web

This feature is not available in the online app; however, you can open the message in Outlook 2016 to use the Live Preview feature.

The Mini Toolbar

The *Mini toolbar* is a floating toolbar that appears when text has been selected in the body of your Outlook message. When you hover over the selected text, the **Mini** toolbar appears; when you move off of the selected text, the **Mini** toolbar disappears.

The **Mini** toolbar contains tools that are commonly used for text formatting, without having to access these tools on the ribbon. The tools in the **Mini** toolbar include:

- Basic font options such as font type, font size, increase font size/decrease font size, and font color.
- Text formatting options such as bold, italics, or underline.
- Paragraph formatting options such as bullet or numbered lists.
- Text highlight color options.
- Format painter, which can be used to copy formatting from one place and apply it to text selected elsewhere.
- Styles that can be applied to the selected text.

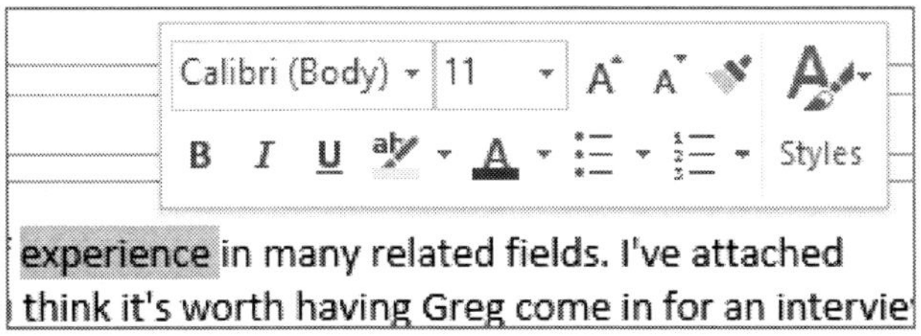

Figure 2-7: The Mini toolbar displays text formatting options for selected text.

Note: Outlook on the Web

This formatting toolbar is also available in the online app; however, there are fewer buttons and they are slightly different in appearance. In addition to the toolbar that appears when text is selected, you can also use the formatting tools located at the bottom of the message area.

Save a Message as a Draft

As you are creating new messages, you can save the current state of the message and complete it at a later time. A saved message is placed in your **Drafts** folder. You can use any of the following methods to save a draft message:

* In the message window, select **File→Save**.
* In the message window, on the **Quick Access Toolbar**, select the **Save** button.
* Select **Ctrl+S** when composing a new message or creating an inline reply.

Note: Outlook on the Web

You can save a message as a draft by selecting the **More commands** button and then selecting **Save draft**. Just as in the desktop application, draft messages are saved in the **Drafts** folder.

Access the Checklist tile on your CHOICE Course screen for reference information and job aids on How to Change Message Format and Apply Formatting.

ACTIVITY 2-3
Formatting Message Content

Data File

C:\091058Data\Formatting Messages\Greg Cover Letter.docx

Before You Begin

Microsoft Word 2016 has been installed on your machine.

Scenario

You have selected the appropriate recipients, composed the message body, and checked the spelling and grammar for your pre-screening email about Greg Shannon to send to the recruitment team. Because this email requires their attention and a response, you also want to make sure that the email is formatted well so that the members of the team can read and respond to it quickly and easily. You especially want to emphasize that you need the team members to respond by tomorrow at the latest.

Part of your message will include a portion of Greg's cover letter to share with the rest of the team, rather than including the whole document for them to read on their own. You will paste this into the email message and make sure it is formatted in the way you want it to be.

1. Enter a line of introduction before the pasted portion of Greg's cover letter.
    a) Select at the end of the text paragraph.
    b) Press **Enter** twice to place two hard returns in the email message.
    c) Type *Here is what Greg had to say about himself in his cover letter:*

2. Format the message content you composed using the **Mini** toolbar.
    a) Select all of the text in the message body. The **Mini** toolbar will appear above the highlighted text.

> **Note:** If you move the cursor away from the highlighted text, the **Mini** toolbar will turn translucent and then disappear. If the **Mini** toolbar is translucent, you can hover over it to make it appear fully and use the toolbar. If it disappears, you will need to select the text again to make it reappear.

    b) In the **Mini** toolbar, select the **Font** drop-down arrow and hover over the available fonts to observe how Live Preview changes the selected text on the screen.
    c) Select **Franklin Gothic Book**.
    d) Select the **Increase Font Size** button A˙ once to increase the font to **12** point size.
    e) In the message body, select only the word **tomorrow** in the first paragraph.
    f) In the **Mini** toolbar, select the **Bold** button. **B**

g) Select the **Font Color** drop-down arrow and in the **Standard Colors** section, select **Dark Red** (the first color from the left in the bottom row).

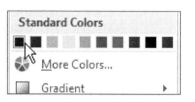

3. Copy and paste a portion of Greg's cover letter into the message body.

   a) Open File Explorer and open the data file **C:\091058Data\Formatting Messages\Greg Cover Letter.docx**.

   b) If you are prompted to switch to Edit mode in the Word document, select **Enable Editing**.

   c) Select and copy the third full paragraph in the document, starting with "I have spent..."

   d) Use the Windows taskbar to switch to the **Greg Shannon info - Message (HTML)** window.

   e) Position the insertion point at the end of the message body and press **Enter** twice.

   f) On the ribbon, select the **Format Text** tab and select the **Paste** drop-down arrow.

   g) Select the second button from the left, **Keep Source Formatting** to paste the content with the formatting from the original document.

4. Indent and apply italic formatting to Greg's cover letter text to differentiate it from your message text.

   a) Verify that your insertion point is somewhere in the paragraph.

   b) On the **Message** tab, in the **Basic Text** command group, select the **Increase Indent** button.

   c) Select the entire paragraph and then select I on either the ribbon or the **Mini** toolbar.

5. On the **Quick Access Toolbar**, select **Save**.
The message is saved in your **Drafts** folder and can be finished and sent at a later time.

6. Close **Greg Cover Letter.docx** and Word without saving changes.

Summary

In this lesson, you learned how to use Outlook features to send professional-looking messages. You used the Address Book to select recipients, checked the spelling of your messages, and applied basic formatting to message text.

Share your stories of how spell check or grammar check increased the professionalism of your email messages.

What type of formatting do you use most often in your messages, and why?

 Note: Check your CHOICE Course screen for opportunities to interact with your classmates, peers, and the larger CHOICE online community about the topics covered in this course or other topics you are interested in. From the Course screen you can also access available resources for a more continuous learning experience.

3 | Working with Attachments and Illustrations

Lesson Time: 1 hour

Lesson Objectives

In this lesson, you will:

- Attach files to messages.

- Add images, SmartArt, and themes to email messages.

- Use stationery, themes, and signatures in messages.

Lesson Introduction

Now that you have selected your recipients, composed and formatted your message, and checked for spelling and grammar, you are ready to send your message. But what if there is other information you want to include with your message, such as a document or file? In this topic, you will attach a file to an email message.

TOPIC A

Attach Files and Items

Sometimes, you may have information that you want to include in your message that cannot be included in the message body. Perhaps you have been working on a document and want to share that document with others for their input or feedback. Rather than pasting the text from that document into your email, you can attach that document to the email for all your recipients to read and review at their convenience.

Attachments

An *attachment* is a document or file that is included and sent along with your email message. A message in the Inbox with the **Paperclip** icon next to it indicates that the message contains an attachment.

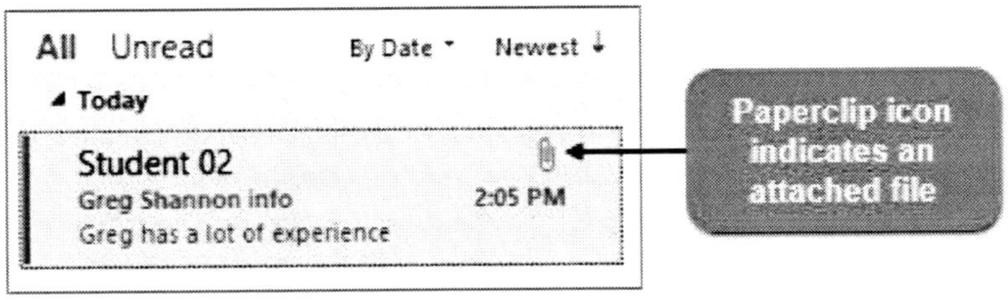

Figure 3-1: The Paperclip icon indicates there is an attachment.

Depending on the message format, the actual attached document will appear in a different location. For HTML or plain text messages, the attachment will appear in a separate **Attached** field beneath the **Subject** field of the email. It will include the file name and type and the file size. For RTF messages, the attachment will appear in the body of the message content. It will display as the **File Type** icon and will include the file name.

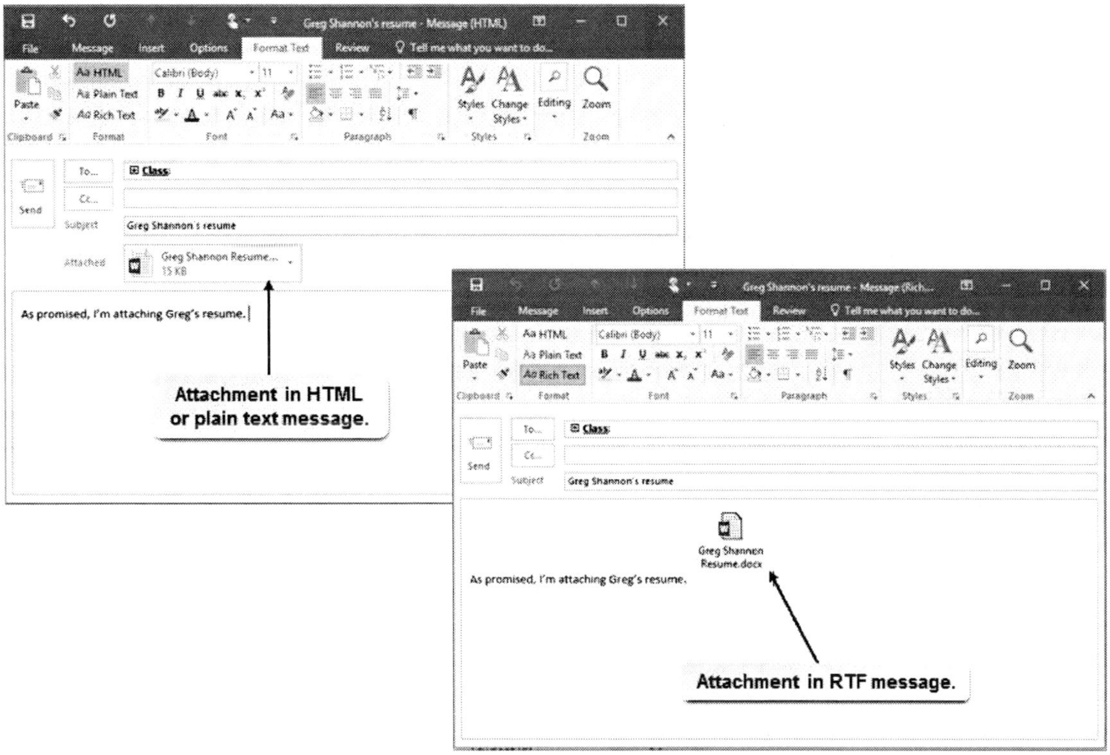

Figure 3-2: Attachments in HTML and RTF messages.

> **Note: Outlook on the Web**
>
> In the online app, you can attach files in the traditional way as a copy or as a linked file that is shared via OneDrive®. The recipient will need to sign in to their Microsoft account (or create an account) before they can view the linked attachment.

Guidelines for File Type and Attachment Size

> **Note:** All of the Guidelines for this lesson are available as checklists from the **Checklist** tile on the CHOICE Course screen.

When sending a file as an attachment, the file type and file size are important factors. Some guidelines you should follow for including attachments in your mail messages are:

* Make sure to attach a file type that your recipients will be able to manage. Not all recipients have the application needed to open and read an attached file.
* The prevalence and free availability of Portable Document Format (PDF) readers ensures that most recipients will be able to open and read a PDF file.
* For less-common and more specific applications, make sure that your recipients can handle the file in its native application. For example, not all recipients will be able to open and work with an Adobe® InDesign® file.
* Be conscious of the size of the file that you are sending. Large attachments require a lot of space and can clog a recipient's Inbox. Make sure to attach files that are small enough for your recipients to be able to manage.
* Some organizations limit the file size for attachments that can be sent or received to prevent an Inbox from reaching capacity. Make sure the file size is not exceeding company limits.
* If you do need to send large files, you may have to send them in multiple messages or use a file compression utility (such as Winzip®) to reduce the file size.

- Another option for sending large files is to find an alternative way to share the files, such as an online drop box or File Transfer Protocol (FTP) site.

Attachment Sources

Attaching documents or other items to your email messages is something you do often, especially if you are using Outlook in a corporate setting where you collaborate on documents frequently. Outlook 2016 makes attaching files even easier, by allowing you to select from a variety of locations and recently accessed files, right from the ribbon in your message.

Now, you can choose to attach a file using the following options:

- From **Recent Items**, you can choose from a list of the last twelve files you most recently accessed. Currently, you cannot delete items from this list or change the number of items shown in this list.
- From **Browse Web Locations**, you can choose from the files you have saved in your OneDrive® or SharePoint® locations.
- From **Browse This PC**, you can choose from the files you have saved to your computer.

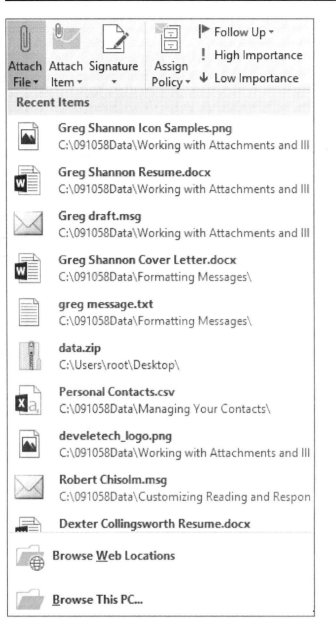

Figure 3-3: The Attach File drop-down list includes all the source options for attaching a file.

Note: Outlook on the Web

Using the online app, you can attach files that are stored on your computer, in Group files, and in OneDrive. After selecting the attachment from the desired source, you will need to specify how you want to attach the file: as a copy or as a OneDrive file. If you choose the OneDrive option, then the file will be uploaded to OneDrive and placed in the **Email Attachments** folder.

Cloud Attachments

Outlook now makes it even easier to share and collaborate on your files using cloud attachments. Using the **Browse Web Locations** option to attach a file to your Outlook message, you can attach a link directly to the most up-to-date files in your OneDrive or SharePoint account. When recipients receive your email with the link, they can open and edit the latest version of the attachment, and then save their changes—right in the cloud.

When you attach a file from the cloud, you can set permissions for the file, and select whether to attach a copy of the file to the email (like a classic attachment) or to share it as a link to the cloud attachment—and choose whether that is a link to an editable version of the file or a viewable version of the file.

Figure 3-4: Changing permissions for the recipient of a cloud attachment.

Outlook Items as Attachments

Outlook items can be attached to your email messages and sent to other recipients. Attaching Outlook items can make it easier to share multiple messages, contacts, tasks, a view of your calendar, and even specific calendar events with others.

> **Note:** While you can send Outlook items to recipients outside your organization who are not using Outlook themselves, not all files will necessarily be compatible with other email clients. Attaching Outlook items works best between users in the same domain, and with recipients using Exchange Server and Outlook.

You can use the commands in the **Include** command group on the **Insert** tab to attach different Outlook items.

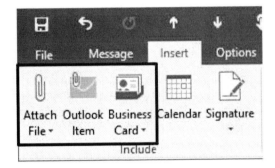

Figure 3-5: The commands to attach Outlook Items to an email message on the Insert tab.

Attached Item	Description
Outlook Item	You can attach an Outlook item such as an email message, meeting invite, or task. When attaching one of these items, you can choose to insert the item as an attachment or as text only, which will appear in the message body. Those who use Outlook should be able to open, save, and interact with these attachments; those using another email client should be able to view the text in the message body, but might not be able to interact directly with the attached file.
Business Card	You can attach a business card with contact information for one or more of your contacts. Along with the file being attached, a view of the business card will display in the message body. Those who use Outlook can view the file and even save it to their own contacts. Those not using Outlook might not be able to interact with the item directly, such as opening or saving the file.
Calendar	You can attach a link to your calendar with information about your meeting events. Along with the link to your calendar, a view of your calendar for a specific date range and with the level of detail of your choice will display in the message body. Those who use Outlook can use the link to open and view your calendar. Those not using Outlook might not be able to interact with the item directly, such as opening and viewing the calendar.

> **Note: Outlook on the Web**
>
> Attaching Outlook items is not available in the online app. To use these options, you must use the desktop application.

Attachment Reminder

Outlook 2016 can detect if an attachment was omitted from a message and notify you that the attachment is missing. Outlook will scan messages before they are sent and look for any indications that you intended to attach a document, such as the word "attachment" in the subject or message text. When Outlook detects that you may have forgotten an attachment, it will display the **Attachment Reminder** dialog box before sending the message.

By default, the Attachment Reminder is enabled in Outlook 2016.

Figure 3-6: The Attachment Reminder dialog box.

Policy Tip

MailTips are at the informative level, sort of a courtesy reminder provided by Outlook. The person sending the email can still choose to send the email.

Policy Tips are different. *Policy Tips* are a form of email security that enforces your organization's email policies. Policy Tips work in the Data Loss Prevention (DLP) security layer within your organization. In other words, if your organization has a policy that prohibits certain types of information to be sent via email, and your organization has defined that policy in its Exchange Server implementation, you will not be able to send the email if it violates the policy.

Policy Tip enforcement levels range from "Notify Only"—where the person sending the email is only notified that, if they send the email, they are violating a specific policy—through "Reject unless explicit override"—where the person sending the email is required to provide justification and get explicit permission to send the email that is violating a policy.

 Note: Policy Tips are only available if your organization is using Exchange Server 2013 or later.

ACTIVITY 3-1
Attaching a File to a Message

Data Files

C:\091058Data\Working with Attachments and Illustrations\Greg Shannon Resume.docx

C:\091058Data\Working with Attachments and Illustrations\Greg draft.msg

Scenario

In your email message to the recruitment team working on screening potential candidates, you provided a little bit of information about Greg Shannon from his cover letter. You decided to attach Greg's résumé to send to the team so that they could all review it on their own time. You need to attach the file to the email message to the recruitment team.

---

1. From the **Drafts** folder, open the **[your initials] Greg Shannon info** email and attach Greg Shannon's résumé to the message.

    a) In the **Folder** pane, select **Drafts**.

     Note: If you do not have the "Greg Shannon info" message in your **Drafts** folder, you can open **C:\091058Data\Working with Attachments and Illustrations\Greg draft.msg**.

    b) On the **Compose Tools→Message** tab, select **Attach File**.

    In Outlook 2016, you can select the file attachment from the list of recently used files, from a web location, or from the files on the local computer.

    c) From the **Attach File** list, select **Browse This PC**.

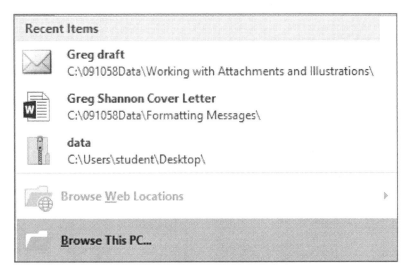

Recent Items

Greg draft
C:\091058Data\Working with Attachments and Illustrations\

Greg Shannon Cover Letter
C:\091058Data\Formatting Messages\

data
C:\Users\student\Desktop\

Browse Web Locations

Browse This PC...

d) In the **Insert File** dialog box, navigate to the C:\091058Data\Working with Attachments and **Illustrations** folder.

e) Select the Word document named **Greg Shannon Resume**.

f) Select **Insert**.

2. Send the email message with the attachment to your recipients.

a) Observe **Attachment** button.

Subject	Greg Shannon info
Attached	[W] Greg Shannon Resume... ▾ 15 KB

The Attachment appears below the subject in the **Attached** field as a button. The button text displays the file icon, name, and file size. You can select the drop-down arrow to open, save, print, or remove the attached file.

b) Select **Send**.

Send

Attachment Options

You have a variety of available actions that can be performed on the attachments you receive. When you select the Attachment in a message, the **Attachment Tools Attachments** contextual tab appears. Additionally, you can select the drop-down arrow on the **Attachment** button to display a shortcut menu. Using either the ribbon or the **Attachment** button, you can perform the following actions: open, print, save, send, remove, and copy the attachment. The **Quick Print** option bypasses the **Print** dialog box.

You can select **Save As** to open the **Save Attachment** dialog box that enables you to save the attachment and specify the name, location, and file type. The **Save Attachment** dialog box resembles the **Save As** dialog box in appearance and function.

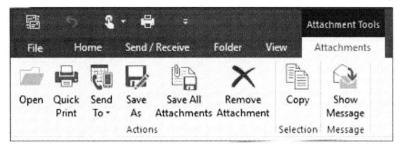

Attachment Tools Attachments ribbon tab

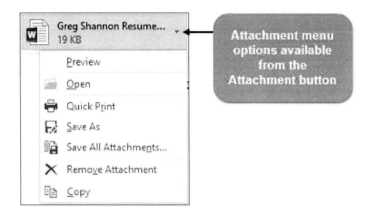

Figure 3-7: The available Attachment options.

Note: Outlook on the Web

When you receive a message containing an attachment, you can view, download, or save the file to OneDrive. If you want to print the attachment, you must first view it and then use the **Print** command. In an Office 365™ for Business account, the previewed attachment appears adjacent to the message on the same browser tab. In a personal account, the attachment opens on a separate browser tab in the applicable Office Online app.

Attachment Preview

The *attachment preview* feature in Outlook allows you to preview a file that has been attached to an email message in the **Reading** pane. With attachment preview, you can view and read attached files without having to open the message from the message list and without having to open the file in its associated application.

Not all file types can be previewed in this manner. For some file types, you might not have the associated file preview software installed. For file types that can potentially contain viruses, such as .bat or .exe files, you will not be able to preview them.

Note: When you preview or open attachments, you may be prompted to only open files from a trustworthy source. If prompted, select **Preview file**. You can choose to ignore this warning for all attachments of the same file type by unchecking **Always warn before previewing this type of file check box before selecting Preview file** option.

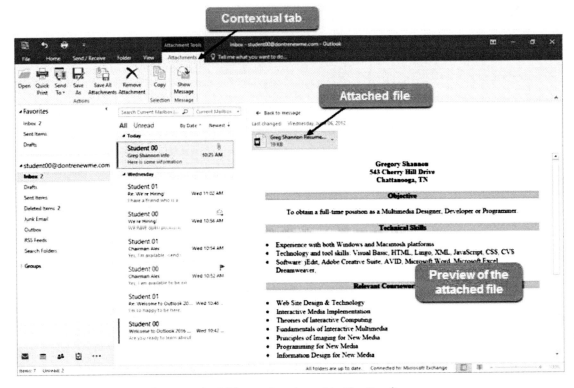

Figure 3-8: A preview of an attached file can be viewed in the Reading pane.

Access the Checklist tile on your **CHOICE** Course screen for reference information and job aids on **How to Attach Files and Outlook Items.**

ACTIVITY 3-2
Working with Received Attachments

Scenario

Since you are part of the recruitment team to hire new employees at Develetech, you have received quite a few emails in your Inbox that include attachments. Recently, most of those attachments have been the résumés of potential candidates. These attachments are starting to clutter up your Inbox and are taking up too much space in your Inbox. You want to print some of these attachments to review as hard copies, save some of the attachments to keep for future reference, and then remove some of the attachments to make more space in your Inbox.

---

1. Preview an attachment in the **Reading** pane.
   a) In your **Inbox** message list, select the email with the Subject: **Greg Shannon info**.
   b) In the **Reading** pane, select the drop-down arrow on the attachment button **Greg Shannon Resume**.

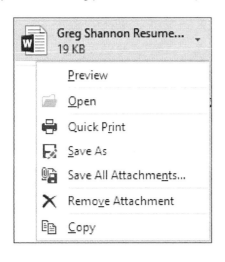

c) Select **Preview**.

> ← Back to message
>
> Last changed: Wednesday, June 6, 2012
>
> [W] Greg Shannon Resume... ▾
>   16 KB
>
> **Gregory Shannon**
> **543 Cherry Hill Drive**
> **Chattanooga, TN**
>
> | Objective |
>
> To obtain a full-time position as a Multimedia Designer, Developer or Programmer.
>
> | Technical Skills |
>
> • Experience with both Windows and Macintosh platforms
> • Technology and tool skills: Visual Basic, HTML, Lingo, XML, JavaScript, CSS, CVS
> • Software: jEdit, Adobe Creative Suite, AVID, Microsoft Word, Microsoft Excel, Dreamweaver,
>
> | Relevant Coursework Completed |
>
> • Web Site Design & Technology
> • Interactive Media Implementation
> • Theories of Interactive Computing

The **Reading** pane now displays a preview of the attached file and not the original message content. Located at the top of the **Reading** pane is a **Back to message** button that will show the message again. Additionally, the contextual **Attachments** tab appears on the ribbon and also contains a **Show Message** button.

2. Save the attachment.

   a) On the **Attachments** tab, select **Save As**.

   b) In the **Save Attachment** dialog box, in the left pane, under **This PC**, select **Desktop**.
   c) Select **New folder** and name the new folder *Resumes*
   d) With the **Resumes** folder selected, select **Open**.
   e) Verify that the **File name** is **Greg Shannon Resume** and select **Save**.
      The Greg Shannon Resume document is now saved in the **Desktop\Resumes** folder.

3. Remove the attachment from the email message to free up space in your Inbox.

   a) From the **Attachment** button drop-down list, select **Remove Attachment**.

b) When prompted to confirm the action, select **Remove Attachment**.

Microsoft Outlook	✕

? Are you sure you want to remove the selected attachment from this message?

[Remove Attachment] [Cancel]

c) Observe that the attachment is no longer attached and the **Reading** pane has returned to showing the message.

TOPIC B

Add Illustrations to Messages

Outlook provides features like themes, styles, illustrations, and pictures that can be added to your emails to make them more visually pleasing, polished, or professional-looking. You can use the features and tools provided in Outlook to enhance your email messages and convey your messages more effectively, while being more aesthetically pleasing. In this topic, you will add illustrations to email messages.

The Illustrations Command Group

The **Illustrations** command group, found on the **Insert** tab of the ribbon in a message form, includes the commands you can use for inserting various graphical elements into your email messages.

Figure 3-9: The Illustrations command group includes commands for inserting various graphical elements into your message.

The graphical elements that can be inserted into a message include:

- **Pictures**
- **Online Pictures**
- **Shapes**
- **SmartArt**
- **Chart**
- **Screenshot**

Note: Outlook on the Web

In the online app, you can insert pictures and Emojis (small icons used to convey emotion) into your messages. To insert any of the other illustrations covered in this topic, you must use the desktop application. However, when you receive messages that contain illustrations, you will be able to see any shapes, SmartArt, charts, and screenshots that have been inserted.

Pictures and Online Pictures

Pictures are inserted from an external source, such as images that have been saved to your local computer. The **Online Pictures** option allows you to search a variety of online sources provided by Outlook to find and insert an image that suits your needs. After inserting a picture from either source, the **Picture Tools Format** ribbon tab provides tools for adjusting the picture size and appearance and how it's arranged in the message.

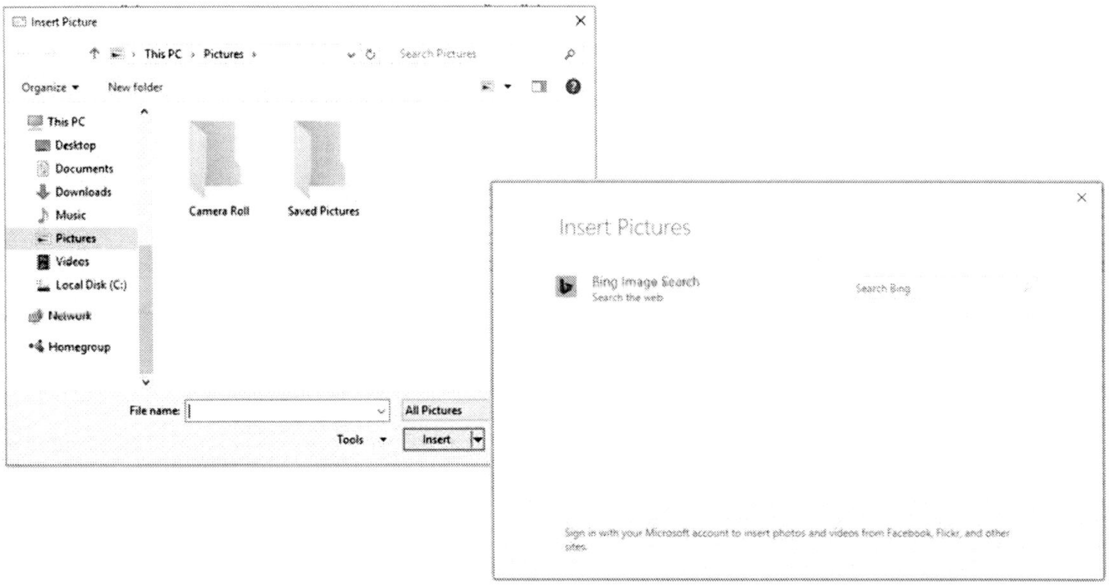

Figure 3-10: Inserting pictures and online pictures.

SmartArt

SmartArt is a tool provided in Outlook and many other Office 2016 applications that lets you format your information into a graphical representation to help convey your message. SmartArt graphics organize your information into a graphical layout that effectively communicates your idea and can be easily understood.

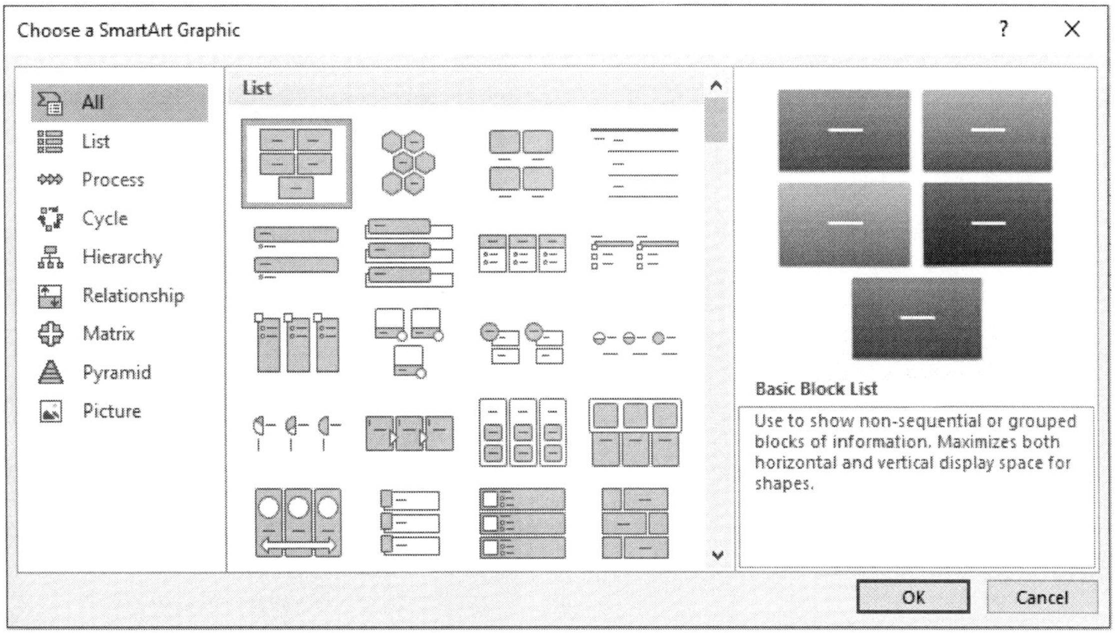

Figure 3-11: SmartArt graphics can organize your information into a number of visual style options.

Each SmartArt graphic is editable and customizable, so you can add your own text, colors, and add, remove, move, or resize shapes as needed. There are a number of SmartArt types that can be applied to your information:

- **List** displays your information as items in a list using graphics.
- **Process** displays your information as a series of steps in a process, such as a flowchart.

- **Cycle** displays your information as a sequence of stages in a cycle, such as a lifecycle.
- **Hierarchy** displays your information as a series of hierarchical relationships, such as an organizational chart.
- **Relationship** displays your information as a series of related pieces, such as a Venn diagram.
- **Matrix** displays your information as parts that make up a whole, such as quadrants of a whole.
- **Pyramid** displays your information relationally or hierarchically where components are building in size, such as an inverted pyramid.
- **Picture** displays your information using a graphical representation, such as an image with callouts.

> **Note:** For a complete description and an example of all the SmartArt types and graphics available, visit **Outlook Help** and search for descriptions of SmartArt graphics.

The Screenshot Tool

The **Screenshot** tool in Outlook is used to capture an image of the screen for any open and available window on your desktop. When you open the **Screenshot** tool, you can choose to capture the entire image of one of your open windows, or you can use the **Screen Clipping** tool to capture a portion of a screen. Once captured, the screenshot is automatically inserted into the message body.

Figure 3-12: The Screenshot Tool captures an image of an available screen on your desktop and inserts it in your email message.

The Text Command Group

The **Text** command group, found on the **Insert** tab of the ribbon in a message form, includes the commands you can use for inserting various graphical text elements into your email messages.

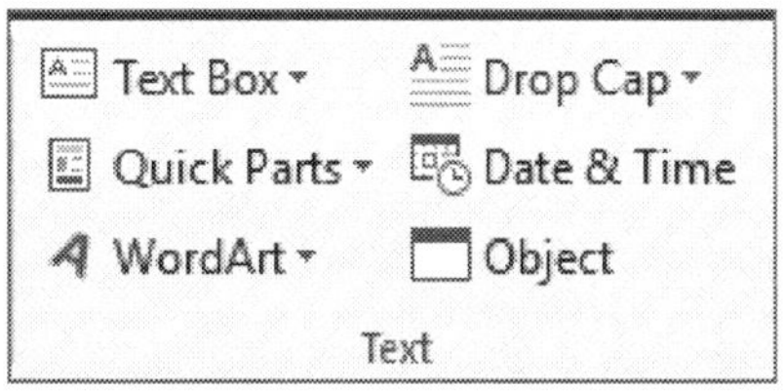

Figure 3-13: Text commands are available for inserting various graphical text elements into your email messages.

The graphical text elements that can be inserted into a message include:

- **Text Box**
- **Quick Parts**
- **WordArt**
- **Drop Cap**
- **Date & Time**
- **Object**

> **Note: Object** allows you to insert any number of other types of files or objects, including video clips, audio clips, and documents from other Microsoft applications.

Quick Parts

You can use the Quick Parts feature to create, save, and reuse pieces of content that you use often, including document titles, author names, and AutoText. *AutoText* is another feature of Outlook that lets you save and reuse words or phrases that you use often; they are added to the AutoText gallery for you to access and insert into an email quickly and easily.

WordArt

Available in the Microsoft Office 2016 applications, *WordArt* is a text-styling feature that allows you to insert and modify text in your email using special effects. WordArt effects include colored outlines, colored fill, and text effects like shadowing, 3-D rotation, and other transform effects. The **Drawing Tools Format** tab appears on the ribbon and can be used to modify the inserted WordArt shape.

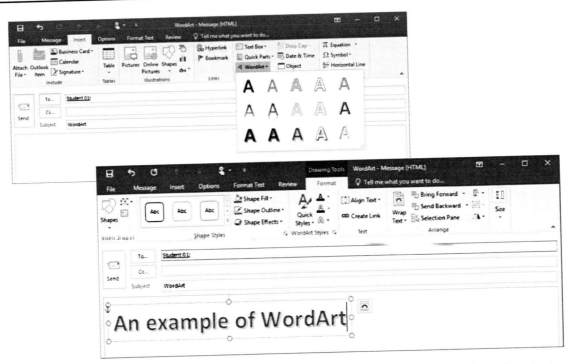

Figure 3-14: WordArt that has been inserted in an email can be modified using the various text effects available.

Contextual Tabs and Tools

Contextual tabs are additional tabs that become available on the ribbon when you insert an object into an email message. These dark blue tabs are displayed to the right of the standard ribbon tabs and display a title that reflects the inserted or selected object, such as Picture, Drawing, SmartArt, and Table.

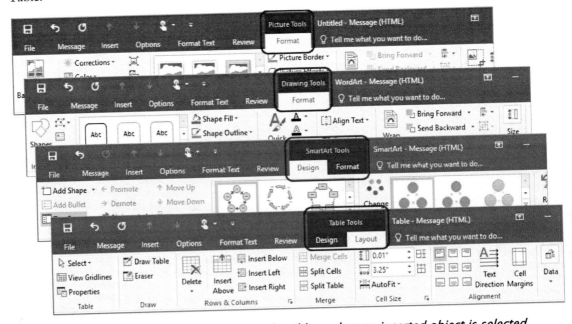

Figure 3-15: The contextual tabs appear on the ribbon when an inserted object is selected.

The available contextual tabs will depend on the selected object and provide commands specific to the selected object. The following table describes the different contextual tabs and a summary of the available tools.

Contextual Tab	Selected Object	Available Tools
Format	• Picture • Shape • SmartArt • Screenshot • Chart	Used to modify the appearance, apply effects, change the size, and adjust the position and alignment of the selected object.
Design	• SmartArt • Table • Chart	Used to change the number of layers, the shape, and layout of the selected object.
Layout	• Table	Used to modify the table properties, the rows and columns, and the cell size and alignment.

Galleries

A *gallery* is a library of all the options that are available for a specific command. If there are many items that can be inserted or formatting options that can be applied, those options are listed in the gallery for that command.

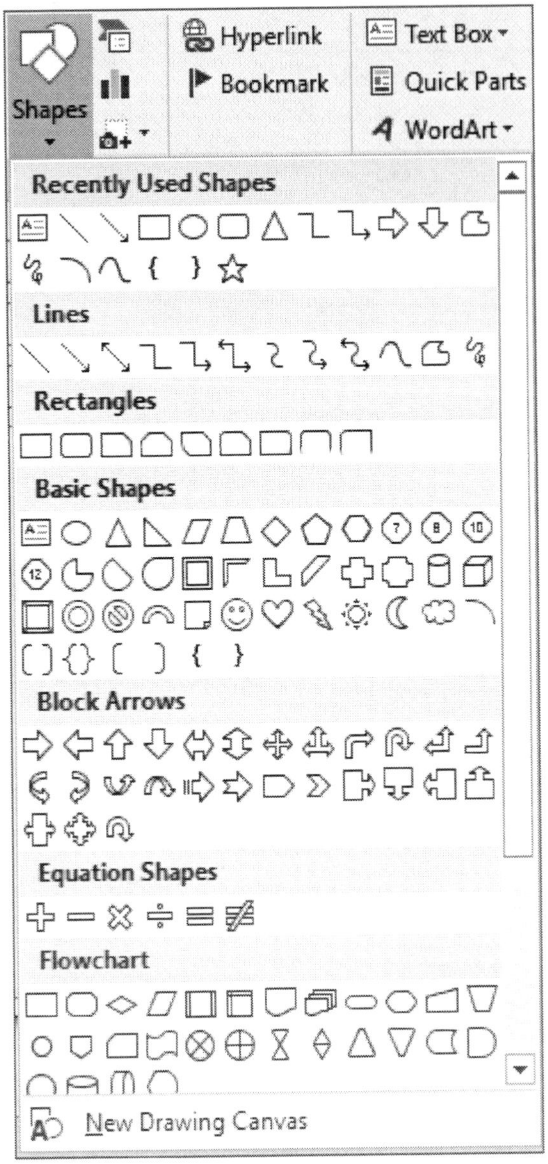

Figure 3-16: The Shapes gallery.

Access the Checklist tile on your CHOICE Course screen for reference information and job aids on How to Insert Illustrations into Messages.

ACTIVITY 3-3
Inserting an Image into an Email Message

Data File

C:\091058Data\Working with Attachments and Illustrations\Icon Samples.png

Scenario

You have decided that you want to include a sample of a Greg Shannon's graphic design work in the email to the recruitment team. You have chosen some sample icons that Greg has created and included in his portfolio of work to use as a sample. You want to insert it into the email as an image so the team can see the samples, without having to open an attachment.

1. Create a new email to send to the team with Greg's sample icons inserted as a picture.

    a) Create a new email message addressed to everyone in the class with the Subject text of *[your name] icon samples*

    b) Select the message body and type *Here's a sample of Greg's work:*

    c) Press **Enter** twice.

    d) Select **Insert** →**Illustrations**→**Pictures**.

    e) In the **Insert Picture** dialog box, navigate to the **C:\091058Data\Working with Attachments and Illustrations** folder and select **Icon Samples.png**.

    f) Select **Insert**.

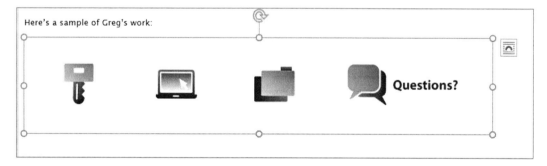

    A collection of icons is inserted into the message body. The **Picture Tools Format** contextual tab appears with commands and buttons that can be used to modify the appearance and positioning of the image.

2. Apply a picture style to the icon samples image to provide a frame-like border.

    a) Maximize the message window.

    b) Verify that the inserted picture is selected.

c) On the **Picture Tools Format** tab, in the **Picture Styles** command group, select a style of your choice.

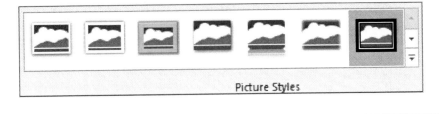

Picture Styles

Note: You can use the up and down scroll arrows or the **More** button to see additional Picture Styles.

The selected style now provides a frame for your icon samples.

3. Send the message.

Styles

Styles are a set of preconfigured formatting options that are available in Outlook. A style may be comprised of formatting options such as font type, font color, paragraph spacing, and more. Rather than spending a lot of time individually formatting your messages, you can use the preconfigured styles to quickly and easily apply formatting to the text.

From the **Styles** command group, simply select the desired style. Or, if the style you want is not visible, you can select the **More** button in the lower-right corner to expand the **Styles** list. You can also display the **Styles** pane by selecting the dialog box launcher in the **Styles** command group.

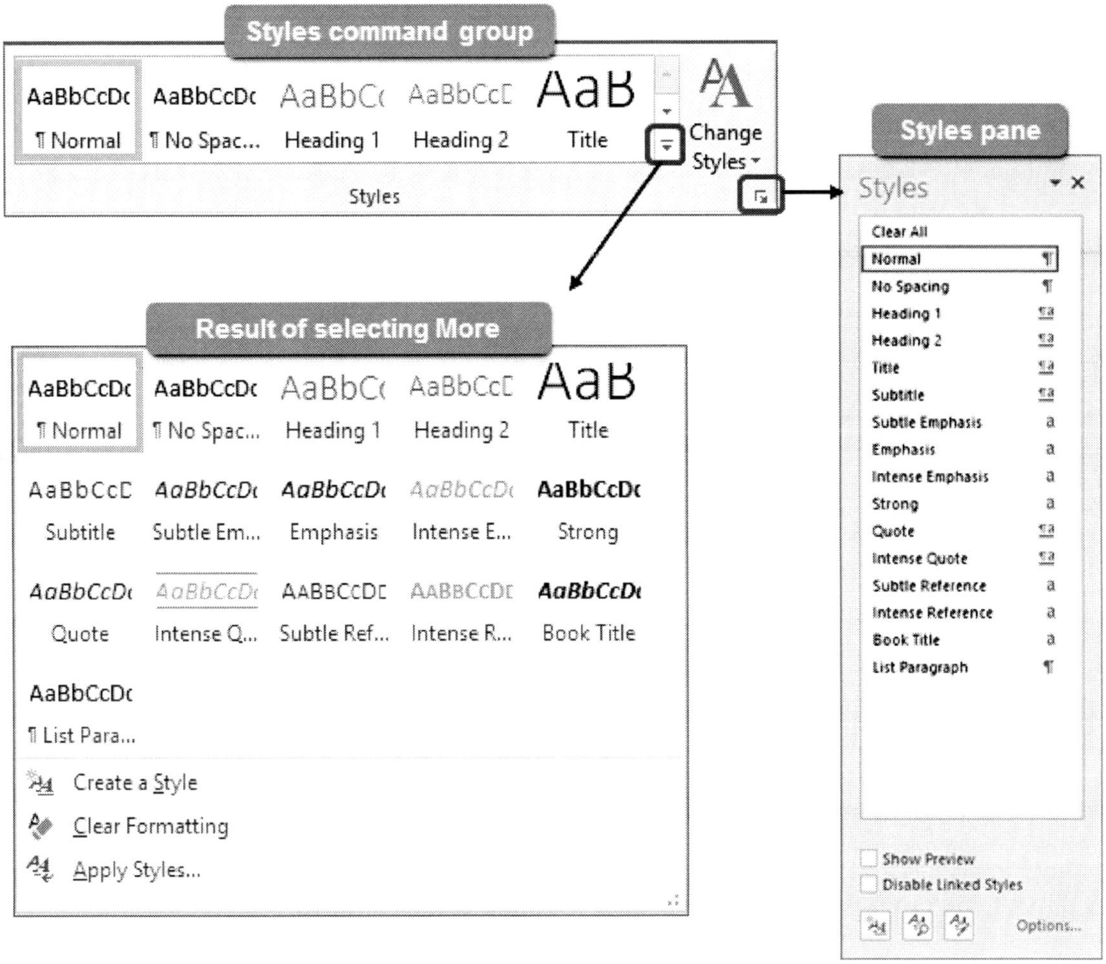

Figure 3-17: Using styles to make formatting changes.

Themes

Themes are preconfigured design and formatting options that can be applied to all message content, from text to graphics and diagrams, to ensure consistency throughout all your message components and give your messages polish and a professional-looking appearance. The theme that is selected specifies the font types that will be used for text in the message, the colors that can be used in the message, and the effects that can be applied to any graphical elements, such as shapes, that are inserted into the message.

There are several themes that are included with the Outlook application. Themes are found on the **Options** tab of the ribbon. You can also customize the existing themes to suit your own personal needs.

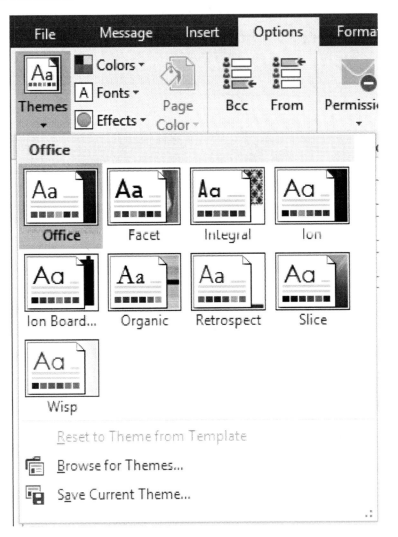

Figure 3-18: The Themes gallery.

Access the Checklist tile on your **CHOICE** Course screen for reference information and job aids on **How to Add Styles and Themes to Messages.**

ACTIVITY 3-4
Using Styles and Themes in Messages

Data File

C:\091058Data\Working with Attachments and Illustrations\About us.txt

Scenario

The marketing director has asked you for a company description that can be added to the marketing pieces. In addition to sending her the text, you'd like to apply some formatting to make it stand out from normal message text.

1. Create a new email message addressed to everyone in class.
   a) Select **New Email**.
   b) In the **To** field, use the Address Book to add the other students in the class.
   c) In the **Subject** field, type *About us*
   d) In the message body, type *Here's a company description for your marketing materials.*

2. Copy all of the text from the **About us.txt** data file and paste it into your **About us** message.
   a) Open File Explorer, and open **C:\091058Data\Working with Attachments and Illustrations\About us.txt**.
   b) Press **Ctrl+A** to select all of the text.
   c) Press **Ctrl+C** to copy the selection.
   d) From the Windows taskbar, activate the **About us** message.
   e) In the message body, press **Ctrl+V** to paste the text on a line after the introductory sentence.

3. Use the **Format Text** tab to apply styles to the pasted text.
   a) Position your insertion point in the line containing **Develetech Industries** and then select **Format Text→Styles→Heading 1**.

> Here's a company description for your marketing materials.
>
> Develetech Industries
> About us

   b) Select **About us** and from the **Styles** list, select **Heading 2**.

> Develetech Industries
> About us

c) Select the bulleted list. Select the **More** button ⊡ and then select the **List Paragraph** style.

A local manufacturer of home electronics, Develetech is a mid-sized company, employing approximately 2,000 residents of Green City and the surrounding area. Develetech is an innovative designer of the following products:

- high-end televisions
- video game consoles
- laptops
- tablets
- mobile phones

The bulleted list is automatically indented.

4. Apply a page color to the message and apply the **Facet** theme.

a) Select **Options→Themes→Page Color** and select a lighter shade of one of the colors.

b) Select **Options→Themes→Themes** and from the available list, select **Facet**.

When you select a different theme, any text with applied styles changes to reflect the new theme colors and fonts, including the page color.

5. Send the message.

6. Close Notepad without saving any changes to the text file.

TOPIC C

Manage Automatic Message Content

You can use graphical elements, themes, and styles to enhance your email messages as needed. But what about including other personal information that you might want to include in every email you send, like your name and contact information? Outlook is equipped with features that let you configure personalized message content like a signature, stationery, and other customized elements that are automatically included on all of your messages. Configuring this automatic message content ensures that your messages are personal and consistent every time you communicate via email.

Outlook Options

By selecting **File→Options**, you can access the global Outlook settings and change them to suit your personal style. In the **Outlook Options** dialog box, you can select any of the categories in the left pane to display additional settings in the right pane. The **Mail** settings enable you to configure how you want Outlook to behave when you are creating, replying to, sending, and receiving messages.

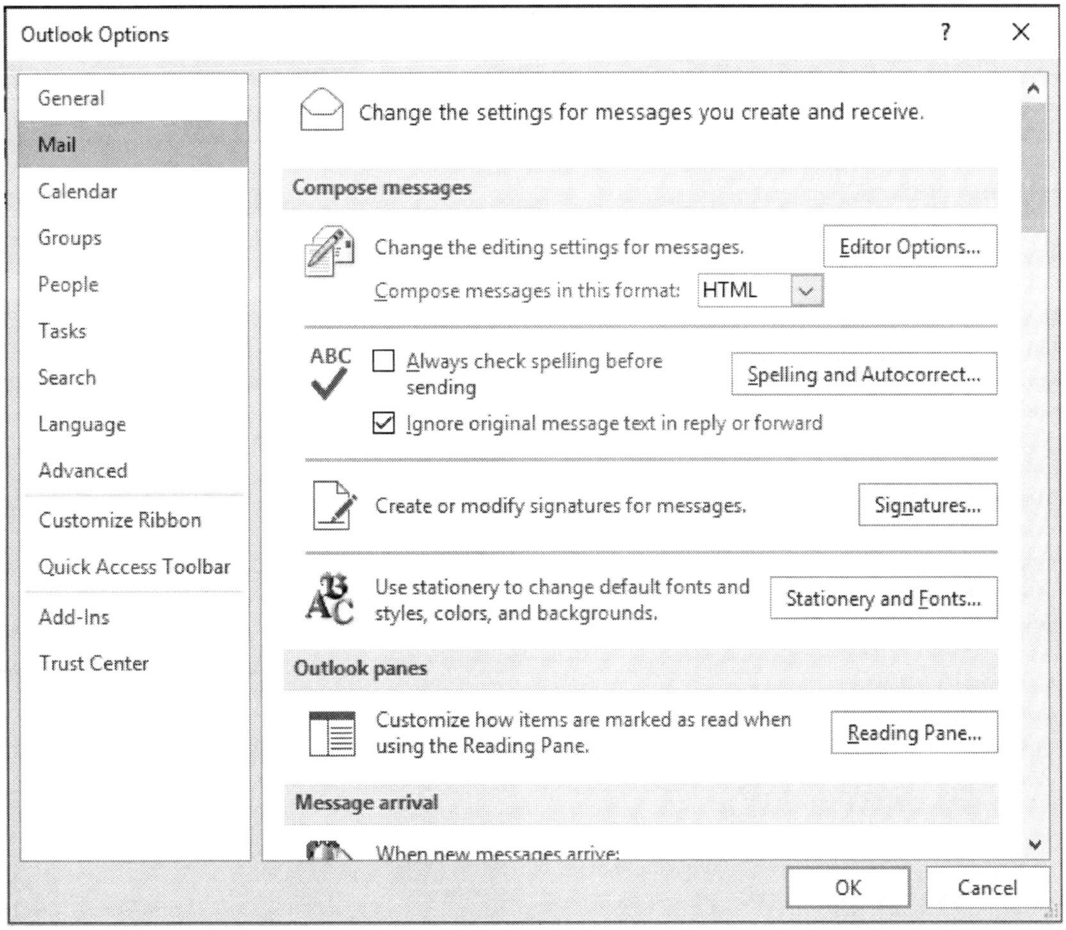

Figure 3-19: The Mail settings in the Outlook Options dialog box.

Note: Outlook on the Web

Using the online app, you can control some of the mail settings that are mentioned here. Instead of using the **Backstage** view, you can access the **Mail** settings by selecting the **Settings** icon ⚙ and then selecting **Mail** to open the **Outlook Options** page.

Stationery and Fonts

The **Stationery** feature provides design templates that you can apply to your HTML-formatted email messages in Outlook. Stationery templates include background colors or patterns that are displayed in the message body of your outgoing messages. Outlook provides a collection of these templates that you can use. You cannot create custom stationery.

There are also theme templates included in Outlook that can be applied to your HTML-formatted email messages. Similar to the themes that are applied to other message components, theme templates include a font and paragraph scheme, and background colors or graphics. You can manipulate theme templates to remove background colors or images and include vivid colors.

Stationery and themes can be selected as a default to be used for all of your new email messages, or you can apply them to a single message of your choice.

Note: Stationery cannot be applied to Rich Text or Plain Text messages, only HTML-formatted messages.

Font Options

Outlook allows you to specify the fonts that will be used when sending, replying to, or forwarding HTML-formatted messages. There are even options to identify comments or change font colors in replies or forward. You can also determine which font will be used when interacting with plain text messages.

To differentiate between multiple responses you have made to the same email thread, you can have Outlook automatically select a new font color for every new response in a thread. Under **Replying or forwarding messages**, check the **Pick a new color when replying or forwarding** check box. Outlook will apply a different font color to each of the multiple responses (replies or forwards) in the thread.

Figure 3-20: The Signatures and Stationery dialog box displays the font options for various types of messages.

Note: Outlook on the Web

You can change the font and basic formatting that will be used in all messages. In other words, you cannot use different fonts for different types of messages.

ACTIVITY 3-5
Changing Font Options

Scenario

You will be sending emails from your Develetech email account both internally within the organization and to external people that you communicate with often. You know that not all of the people you communicate with via email will be able to receive HTML-formatted messages. You want to specify the font options for the various message formats so that all of your recipients receive professional-looking emails from you.

1. Open the **Personal Stationery** dialog box where you will specify your font options.
   a) In the Outlook window, select **File→Options**.
   b) In the **Outlook Options** dialog box, select **Mail**.
   c) In the **Compose messages** section, select **Stationery and Fonts**.

   The **Signatures and Stationery** dialog box opens with the **Personal Stationery** tab selected.

2. Specify **Garamond, Regular, 12 pt** font for new mail messages.
   a) In the **New mail messages** section, select the **Font** button.

   New mail messages
   Font...
   Replying or forwarding messages

   b) In the **Font** field, select **Garamond**.

   > **Note:** With the **Font** list selected, you can type the first letter of the font name to quickly scroll the list to fonts beginning with that letter.

   c) In the **Font** style field, select **Regular**.
   d) In the **Size** field, select **12**.

   Preview

   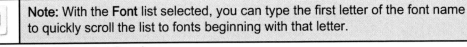
   Sample Text

   This is a TrueType font. This font will be used on both printer and screen.

   The **Preview** box displays your selected font choice.
   e) Select **OK**.

3. Specify **Garamond, Regular, 12 pt** font in **Blue** for replies or forwards.
   a) In the **Replying or forwarding messages** section, select the **Font** button.
   b) In the **Font** field, scroll down in the list to find and select **Garamond**.

c) In the **Font** style field, select **Regular**.

d) In the **Size** field, select **10**.

e) From the **Font color** drop-down list, select **Blue, Accent 1, Darker 50%**, as shown.

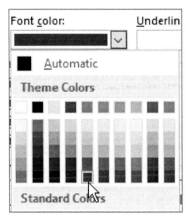

f) Select **OK**.

g) Select the **Mark my comments with** check box and replace the default text with your initials.

Replying or forwarding messages	
Font... _____	Sample Text
☑ Mark my comments with:	SO1
☐ Pick a new color when replying or forwarding	

h) Select **OK** twice to save your font choices.

4. Create email messages to observe your selected font options.

a) Create a new email addressed to everyone with the Subject *[your name] font test*

b) In the message body, type *This is my new font* and on the ribbon, observe the **Basic Text** command group.

Garamond ▾ 12 ▾ A˄ A˅ ☰ ▾ ☰ ▾ ✖
B I U ᵃᵇ⁄ ▾ A ▾ ☰ ☰ ☰ ☲ ☲
Basic Text

The default font settings (Garamond, Regular, 12 pt) are the ones that you recently defined.

c) Send the message.

d) In your Inbox message list, select one of the **font activity** messages you've just received and select **Reply All**.

e) Type a reply of your choice and observe the font appearance.

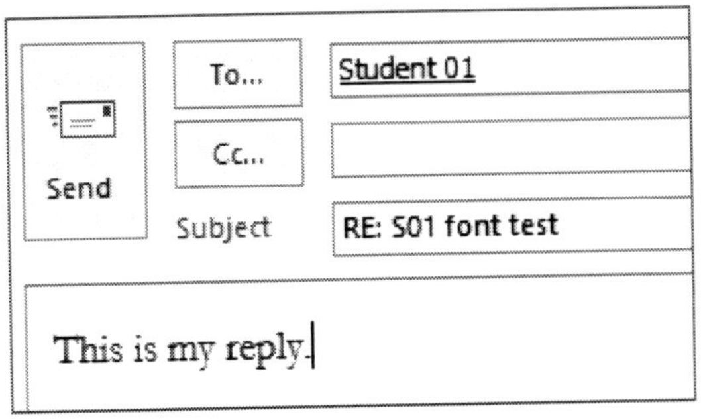

As defined earlier, the font settings are Garamond, Regular, 12 pt, and the font color is blue.

f) Send the reply.

Signatures

A *signature* is a standard closing element that can be created, personalized, and then added to the end of your email messages. The signature identifies the sender of the email message, and usually includes the sender's name and contact information and possibly a picture, such as a company logo. A signature can also include hyperlinks that will open linked content, such as a link to a company website.

You can create multiple signatures that you can append to your email messages for different needs. You can append your signature to an email message manually, or you can configure the option to add your signature to your emails automatically. By default, a signature is not automatically added to your messages.

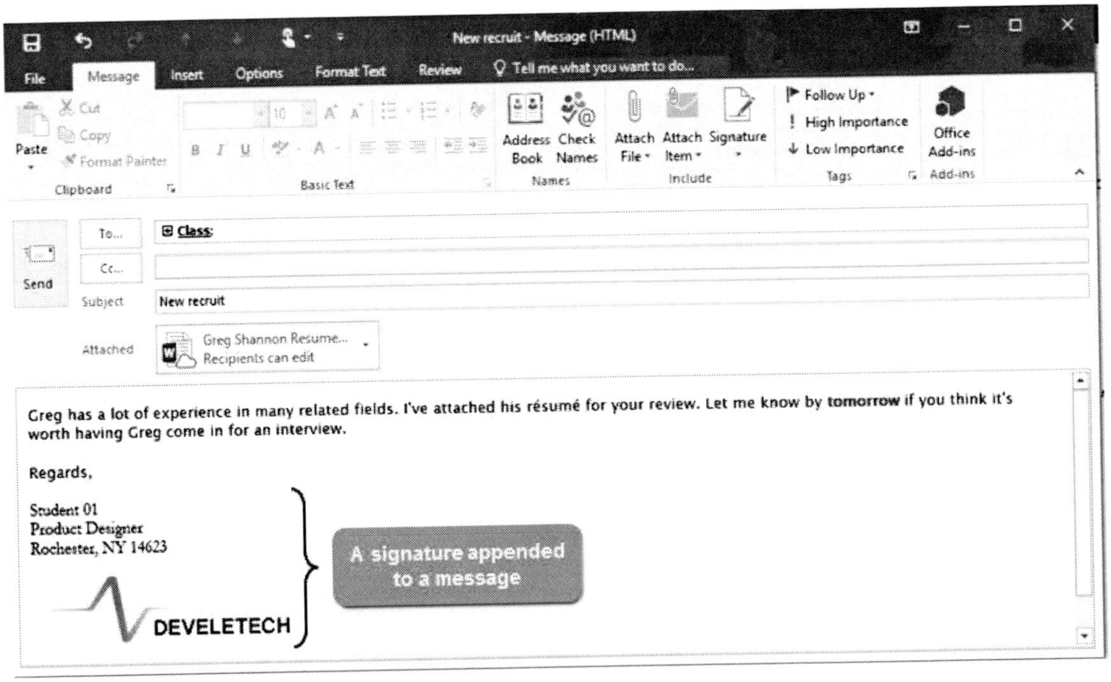

Figure 3–21: A signature appended to the end of an email message.

Note: Outlook on the Web

You have access to your email signature by opening the **Outlook Options** page from the **Settings** pane. From the **Options** list on the left, select **Mail→Layout→Email signature**. You have a variety of formatting options available and can also specify which types of messages you want the signature applied to.

Access the Checklist tile on your CHOICE Course screen for reference information and job aids on **How to Manage Stationery, Themes, and Signatures.**

ACTIVITY 3-6
Creating and Applying an Email Signature

Data File

C:\091058Data\Working with Attachments and Illustrations\logo.png

Scenario

Now that Develetech is using Outlook as the email application for the organization, all employees have been instructed to create and apply a signature to their emails. Human Resources has asked that everyone create an email signature that includes some basic information about themselves such as their name, job title, and contact information and include the Develetech logo. Once you create your signature, you will need to apply it to your outgoing messages.

1. Create a new signature named **Develetech**.
   a) Select **File→Options**.
   b) In the **Outlook Options** dialog box, select **Mail**.
   c) Select **Signatures**.
   d) In the **Signature and Stationery** dialog box, in the **Select signature to edit** section, select **New**.
   e) In the **New Signature** dialog box, type *Develetech* and select **OK**.

2. Compose and format your signature text.
   a) In the **Edit signature** box, type your name.
   b) On a new line, type *Product Designer* and use the **Bold** button to apply bold formatting. Press **Enter**.
   c) On a new line, type your city, state, and zip code.

   d) Select and highlight the entire signature text, and from the **Font Type** drop-down list, select **Garamond**.

3. Insert the Develetech logo (logo.png) at the bottom of your signature.
   a) Below the signature text of name, title, and location, add a blank line.
   b) Select the **Picture** button.
   c) In the **Insert Picture** dialog box, navigate to the **C:\091058Data\Working with Attachments and Illustrations** folder.
   d) Select the **logo.png** file.

e) Select **Insert** and deselect the logo image.

Student 01
Product Designer
Rochester, NY 14623

DEVELETECH

4. Apply the new signature to all your outgoing messages.
   a) In the **Choose default signature** section, in the **New messages** field, select **Develetech**.
   b) From the **Replies/forwards** drop-down list, select **Develetech**.

Choose default signature

E-mail account:	student01@develetechindustry.onmicrosoft.com
New messages:	Develetech
Replies/forwards:	Develetech

   c) Select **OK** to close the **Signatures and Stationery** dialog box.
   d) Select **OK** to close the **Outlook Options** dialog box.

5. Create a new email to verify that your signature is automatically added to the bottom of the message.
   a) On the **Home** tab, select **New Email** and verify that your signature appears in the message body.
   b) Address the email to everyone in the class with the **Subject** *[your_name] signature*
   c) Send the message.

Summary

In this lesson, you composed more sophisticated email messages using attachments and automatic content. Knowing how to use all of the features of Outlook that are available to you can help you compose more complex and professional email messages.

Which of the available Outlook attachment and illustration features have you used in the past or do you think you would use in future email communications? Why?

What are some of your experiences with attaching files or items to your emails?

 Note: Check your CHOICE Course screen for opportunities to interact with your classmates, peers, and the larger CHOICE online community about the topics covered in this course or other topics you are interested in. From the Course screen you can also access available resources for a more continuous learning experience.

4 Customizing Message Options

Lesson Time: 45 minutes

Lesson Objectives

In this lesson, you will:

- Customize reading options.

- Customize message responses with voting and tracking options.

- Recall and resend previously sent messages.

Lesson Introduction

Other than composing new emails to send to your recipients, the other two actions that you are likely to perform most often are reading and responding to emails that you receive. In this lesson, you will learn how to use the available reading and responding options.

TOPIC A

Customize Reading Options

Chances are, if you are using Microsoft® Office Outlook® 2016 in a business organization, you will receive and read numerous emails every day. Opening and reading every email that comes into your Inbox can be time-consuming. Fortunately, you can customize your reading options in Outlook to help you maximize your time reading and responding to emails. In this topic, you will customize these reading options.

Desktop Alerts

Desktop alerts are notifications that appear on-screen when a new Outlook item, such as an email message or meeting invitation, is delivered to your Inbox. When a new item is received, a small alert will appear in the lower-right corner of your screen, on top of any open windows.

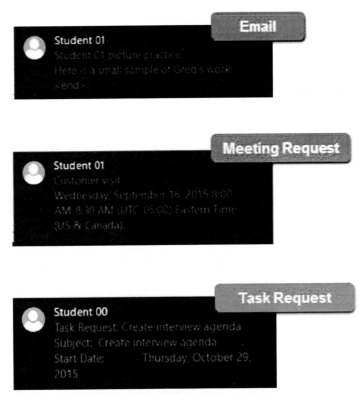

Figure 4-1: A desktop alert appears on-screen when a new Outlook item arrives.

In addition to displaying the sender and the subject line, the other information depends on the type of alert.

- For an email message, the first line of the message is also included.
- For a meeting request, the date, time, and location of the meeting is also included.
- For a task request, the task start date is also included.

By default, desktop alerts are turned on, but you can turn off desktop alerts and all other forms of message arrival notifications if desired.

Other Message Arrival Notifications

Any combination of desktop alerts and notifications can be configured to best notify or remind you of new items in your Inbox. There are other notifications that you can set to notify you when a new item arrives. These notifications include:

- Playing a sound.
- Briefly changing the appearance of the cursor (if applicable).
- Showing an envelope in the taskbar until the email is marked as read.

> **Note: Outlook on the Web**
>
> When you receive new mail, a notification will appear in the upper-right corner of your browser window. Like the desktop alert in the desktop application, the notification box appears for a brief moment and you can select it to open the message in a separate browser window.

Pane Views

Views are options that you can use to control how information is displayed in Outlook. You can manipulate the views of the various panes that make up the Outlook window—the **Folder** pane, the **Content** pane, the **Reading** pane, and the **To-Do Bar**—to suit your personal preferences and make viewing your Outlook items easier. You can arrange the panes of the Outlook window with the commands available on the **View** tab on the ribbon.

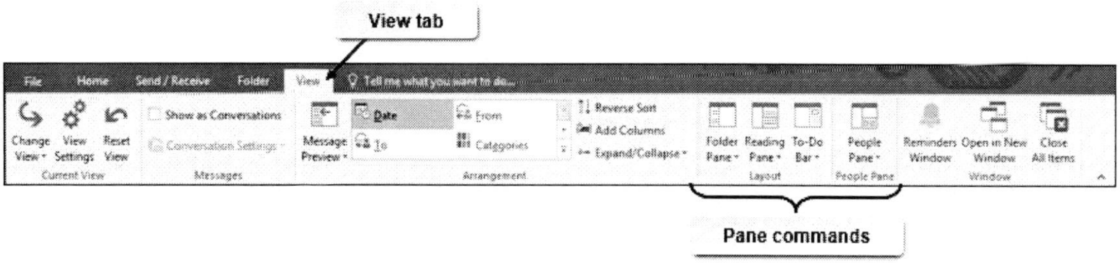

Figure 4-2: The View tab.

- The **Folder** pane can be minimized or turned off to provide more space for the **Content** pane and the **Reading** pane.
- By default, the **To-Do Bar** is turned off.
- The **Reading** pane can be docked either to the right of the **Content** pane or at the bottom of the **Content** pane, or it can be turned off altogether.
- The **Content** pane can be configured to display the items in various ways, including how items are arranged or sorted, which columns are displayed for items, and other advanced settings for the view selected.

> **Note: Outlook on the Web**
>
> To control the width of the **Folder** pane, you can simply drag the right border to the desired size. To change the display settings, you can select the **Settings** icon and then select **Display settings**. Using this link, you will have access to settings for the **Reading** pane, **Message list**, and **Conversations**. Select the desired category to make changes to those settings.

Message Preview

Message Preview is a feature in Outlook that displays the first few lines of a message in the **Content** pane, beneath the subject line of the message. Message Preview lets you read the beginning portion of the message to get an idea of what the message is about, without having to open the message in the **Reading** pane or in a new Outlook window.

By default, Message Preview is enabled, and displays one line of text from the message body. You can choose to modify the Message Preview to display up to three lines of text, or you can choose to disable the feature based on your personal preferences.

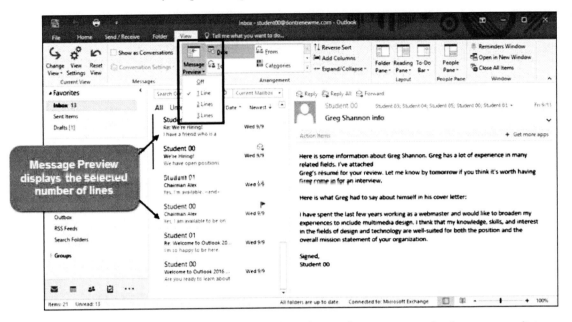

Figure 4-3: Message Preview can display up to three lines of message text in the message list.

Conversations

Messages that you receive that are all part of the same thread of discussion and that share the same subject matter can be organized in Outlook using *conversations*. When conversations in Outlook are enabled, all messages that you have sent or received and which have the same subject line are grouped together with the subject line as the heading. When multiple messages are being sent back and forth between multiple people concerning the same subject matter, conversations can be a useful tool in organizing and managing these messages in your Inbox.

Conversations in your Inbox are identified with a right-pointing triangle ▷ at the far left of the most recent email message you have received in the conversation thread. The entire message thread can be collapsed or expanded to hide or display all of the messages in the conversation thread. When a new email is received within the conversation, the entire conversation is moved to the top of your Inbox. If a conversation contains any unread messages, the most recent message in the conversation thread will display the colored bar to the left of the message and the blue, bold subject heading.

> **Note:** Conversations can include messages across multiple folders in your Outlook environment. For instance, items you send are saved in your **Sent Items** folder, but when conversations are enabled, you will also see those items within the conversation. If you move messages that are part of a conversation to folders you have created within Outlook, while those messages will be saved and stored in that folder, they will also appear in your Inbox as part of that conversation.

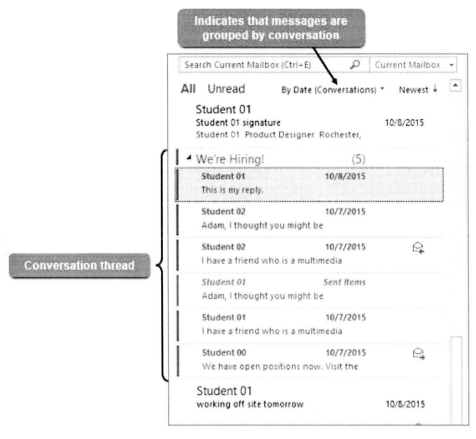

Figure 4-4: A conversation displays multiple messages regarding the same subject.

Split Conversations

A conversation can have more than one message thread within it; a conversation with multiple threads is called a split conversation. Split conversations may occur when someone replies to an earlier message rather than the latest message, forwards a message to a new recipient, or replies to only one person in a multiple-recipient thread.

> **Access the Checklist tile on your CHOICE Course screen for reference information and job aids on How to Customize Your Reading Options for Messages.**

ACTIVITY 4-1
Customizing Your Reading Options

Scenario

Now that you have been working with mail for a little while, you have found that the default reading options do not suit your preferences. You want to customize your Mail view and your reading options so that you can interact with the messages in your Inbox quicker and more efficiently.

1. Remove the **Favorites** section from displaying in the **Folder** pane.
   a) On the ribbon, select the **View** tab.
   b) In the **Layout** command group, select **Folder Pane** and from the drop-down list, select **Minimized**.

c) Observe the minimized **Folder** pane.

The **Folder** pane is collapsed and the folder names and **Navigation** icons are displayed vertically.

d) At the top of the **Folder** pane, select the **Expand** button [›] and then select [📌] to pin it.

 Note: You can also use the ribbon button to return the **Folder** pane to its expanded state. To do so, select **View→Layout→Folder Pane→Normal**.

2. Change the location of the **Reading** pane.

a) Select **View→Reading Pane**.

Reading Pane ▾

b) From the drop-down list, select **Bottom**.
The **Content** pane is now divided horizontally and the **Reading** pane is located at the bottom. Your message list appears in the top half of the window and the column headings are now visible.

3. Modify how the columns are displayed in the message list by removing the **Size** column and changing the position of the **Attachments** column.

a) On the ribbon, on the **View** tab, in the **Arrangement** command group, select the 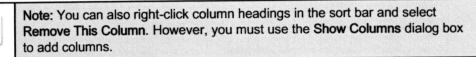 button.

b) In the **Show these columns in this order** box, select **Size**.

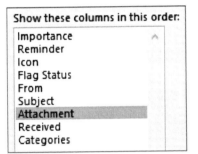

c) Select the <-**Remove** button.

> 🗒 **Note:** You can also right-click column headings in the sort bar and select **Remove This Column.** However, you must use the **Show Columns** dialog box to add columns.

d) In the **Show these columns in this order** box, select **Attachment**.

e) Select Move **Down** twice to place the **Attachment** column between **Subject** and **Received**.

Show these columns in this order:

Importance
Reminder
Icon
Flag Status
From
Subject
Attachment
Received
Categories

f) Select **OK**.

g) Verify that the columns in your message list have changed.

4. Change the arrangement of the items in your message list.

a) In the **Arrangement** command group, select **From**.

📅 Date	📧 From	📧 To
▦ Categories	▸ Flag: Start Date	▸ Flag: Due Date

Your message list is now sorted and arranged by the message sender in the **From** column.

b) Select **Date** to sort and arrange messages by the **Date** column.

> 🗒 **Note:** You can also select the column heading to quickly sort and arrange the messages based on that column.

5. Show the message list arranged by conversations.

a) On the **View** tab, in the **Messages** command group, select **Show as Conversations**.

b) Turn off the **Reading Pane**.

c) Observe the conversation symbols ▷ in the message list.

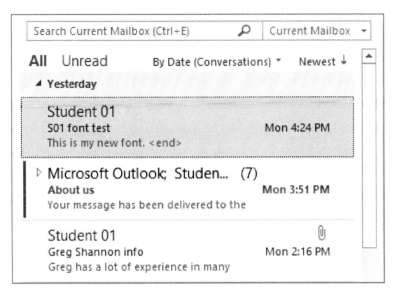

When messages are shown as conversations, the white arrows indicate that additional messages exist and have been collapsed with the most recent message displayed. If any of the messages in the thread are unread, then the most recent message will appear unread.

6. Configure the notifications you will receive when new items arrive in your Inbox.

   a) On the ribbon, select the **File→Options**.

   b) In the **Outlook Options** dialog box, select **Mail**.

   c) In the **Message arrival** section, uncheck the **Play a sound** check box and verify that **Briefly change the mouse pointer** check box is unchecked.

Message arrival

When new messages arrive:

☐ Play a sound

☐ Briefly change the mouse pointer

☑ Show an envelope icon in the taskbar

☑ Display a Desktop Alert

　　☐ Enable preview for Rights Protected messages (May impact performance)

---

   d) Leave the last two options, **Show an envelope icon in the taskbar** and **Display a Desktop Alert** checked.

   e) Select **OK** to save your settings.

7. Customize the layout of your **Mail** view to suit your working style.

TOPIC B

Track Messages

Often, you are using email to communicate important information. You want to make sure that your emails are sent successfully, read in a timely manner, and include all the information you need to convey. You can use the features available in Outlook—such as voting and tracking—to help you manage your message responses.

The InfoBar

The InfoBar is a banner that appears near the top of an open or selected Outlook item, below the ribbon in an open item and below the subject and sender in the **Reading** pane, and provides information about the item.

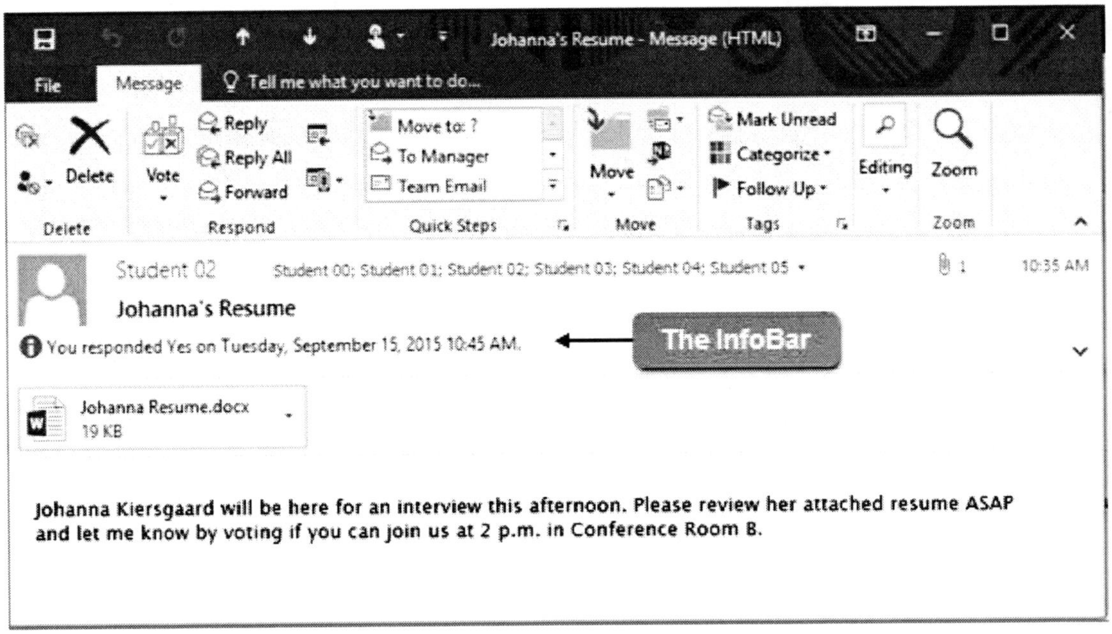

Figure 4-5: The InfoBar provides information about the selected item.

Depending on the type of item, the InfoBar might display:

- The date and time you replied to or forwarded an email.
- If a message has been flagged for follow up.
- If a message has been categorized with a color category.
- The date and time you responded to a meeting invite, and how you responded (accepted, denied, tentatively accepted, and more).
- Other information about the item, such as if extra line breaks were removed from a message.

Voting Options

Located on the **Options** tab in the **Tracking** command group, the **Use Voting Buttons** drop-down list lets you send an email to your recipients that includes a simple poll. You can choose from simple Approve/Reject; Yes/No; or custom response options.

Figure 4-6: Adding voting options to an email.

When you include voting options in an email, the InfoBar displays text telling the recipients to vote; recipients can then select and send their choice via an email response. The results can be tracked in your message list.

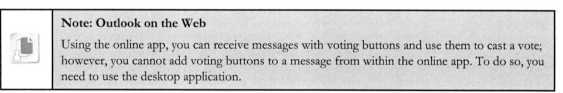

Figure 4-7: The InfoBar provides instructions on how to vote.

> **Note: Outlook on the Web**
>
> Using the online app, you can receive messages with voting buttons and use them to cast a vote; however, you cannot add voting buttons to a message from within the online app. To do so, you need to use the desktop application.

Tracking Options

Located on the **Options** tab, in the **Tracking** command group, the tracking options provided in Outlook follow the actions taken on emails you send, whether a new message or a reply message.

The **Request a Delivery Receipt** option can be enabled for an email to keep track of when the email was delivered. If this option is enabled, you will receive a message from Microsoft Outlook notifying you that your message was delivered successfully.

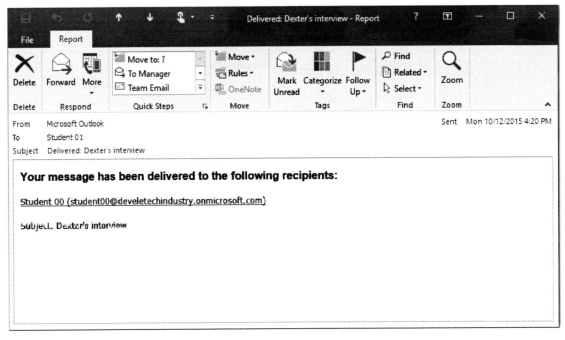

Figure 4-8: A delivery receipt notifies you that your email has been delivered.

The **Request a Read Receipt** option can be enabled for an email to keep track of if and when your email was read by the intended recipient. If this option is enabled, you will receive a message from the recipient notifying you that your message was read.

> **Note:** When you enable read receipts, the recipient is notified that you have requested a read receipt for the email. The recipient can choose whether or not to send the confirmation notification. They can also choose to ignore all read receipts requested of them.

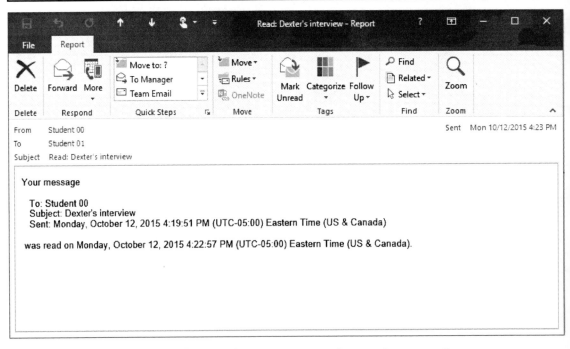

Figure 4-9: A read receipt notifies you that your recipient has read your email.

Note: For more information about using the read receipt option to track an email, check out the LearnTO **Track an Email Using Read Receipts** presentation from the **LearnTO** tile on the CHOICE Course screen.

Note: Outlook on the Web

You can request delivery receipts and read receipts to messages by selecting **More commands→Show message options** to open the **Message options** dialog box. You can also set the **Sensitivity** of the message in this same dialog box.

Access the Checklist tile on your CHOICE Course screen for reference information and job aids on How to Use Voting and Tracking Options.

ACTIVITY 4-2
Using Voting and Tracking Options

Data File

C:\091058Data\Customizing Message Options\Johanna Resume.docx

Scenario

You need to organize a meeting of the recruitment team. Your message is very important and includes information that you need to make sure the team receives. You want to make sure that it will be delivered successfully, so you want to use the tracking options in Outlook to be notified that it has been delivered.

1. Compose an email about Johanna Kiersgaard's interview to the recruitment team.
   a) Create a new message and address it to everyone in class.
   b) In the **Subject** field, type *Johanna's Resume*
   c) In the message body, type *Johanna will be here for an interview this afternoon. Please review her attached resume ASAP and let me know by voting if you can join us at 2 p.m. in Conference Room B.*

   > **Note:** Remember that you do not have to type this text verbatim, and you can type other text if it is appropriate.

2. Attach Johanna's resume to the email.
   a) Select the **Insert** tab and then select **Attach File→Browse this PC**.
   b) Attach **C:\091058Data\Customizing Message Options\Johanna Resume.docx** to the email.

3. Add voting buttons and track the delivery of your email message.
   a) On the ribbon, select the **Options** tab.
   b) In the **Tracking** command group, select **Use Voting Buttons→Yes;No**.

The InfoBar displays that you've added voting buttons.

> ⓘ You added voting buttons to this message.

   c) In the **Tracking** command group, select the **Request a Delivery Receipt** check box.

4. Select **Send** to send the message with your voting buttons and tracking option enabled.

5. Verify that you receive your tracking notifications.

   a) Verify that you receive a message from Microsoft Outlook with the Subject **Delivered: Johanna's Resume**.

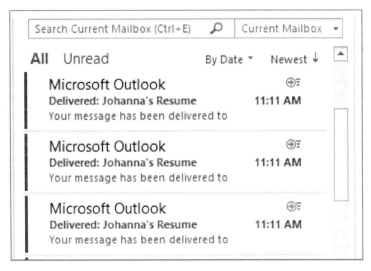

> 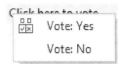 **Note:** It may take a few minutes to receive the delivery receipt, depending on how quickly the Microsoft Exchange Server can process and send the notification.

   b) In the **Quick Access Toolbar**, select **Send/Receive All Folders** 📧 to refresh your message list.

6. Open one of the **Johanna Resume** messages that was sent to you by another student and respond by voting.

   a) In the message list, select one of the **Johanna's Resume** messages that you received.

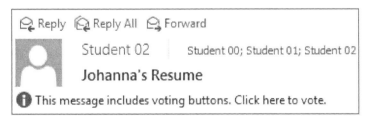

   At the top of the **Reading pane**, the InfoBar notifies you that the message includes voting buttons.

   b) As instructed, select the message to display the voting buttons, and cast your vote.

   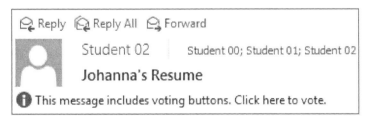

   After voting, you have the option to send your response immediately or edit the response before sending.

c) Select **OK** to send the response without editing it.

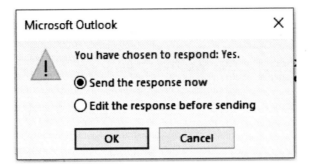

d) Observe the InfoBar message that displays how and when you voted.

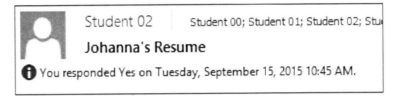

e) Observe how others voted as their responses are delivered to your Inbox.

TOPIC C

Recall and Resend Messages

At this point, you've sent your messages with the desired tracking options so you can stay informed about the delivery and receipt status. However, what if you decide that you forgot to include an important bit of information in a message? What if you receive a tracking notification that the message wasn't delivered to its recipient? In this topic, you'll learn how to use the resend and recall options to work with messages that have already been sent.

Note: Outlook on the Web

The advanced message options discussed in this topic are only available in Outlook 2016.

The Resend Option

There may be times when you need or want to resend a message that you have already sent. Perhaps you forgot to include a recipient or need to add a recipient, or received a tracking notification that your message was not successfully sent. The resend option in Outlook allows you to resend your email messages easily and quickly. To access the **Resend This Message** command, you will need to open the message in a separate window.

Figure 4-10: The resend option is available for sent messages in Outlook.

The Recall Option

There may be times when you need or want to recall a message that you have already sent. Perhaps you sent a message to the wrong person, sent the message too soon and need to revise the information, or forgot to attach a file. If the message has not yet been read by any of your recipients, you can use the recall option in Outlook to stop the delivery of your message altogether or, if desired, stop the delivery of the message and replace it with a new message. To access the **Recall This Message** command, you will need to open the message in a separate window.

Note: The recall option is only available when Outlook is being used with Exchange Server, and only for emails sent to Exchange Server accounts. The Exchange Server can be an on-premise server, or you can be accessing an Exchange Server through Office 365. You will not be able to recall messages that you sent to email addresses outside of your organization or using other email clients.

Figure 4-11. Recalling a message.

 Note: Both the resend and recall options are only available if you save and store your sent items. By default, copies of your sent messages are saved in your **Sent Items** folder. You can change the global Save message settings or change the location on a message-by-message basis using the **Save Sent Item To** command on the **Options** tab in the message form for an unsent message.

Access the Checklist tile on your CHOICE Course screen for reference information and job aids on How to Resend or Recall Messages.

ACTIVITY 4-3
Recalling a Sent Message

Scenario

You are sending numerous emails to the recruitment team, and sometimes you send them with mistakes and without including all the information. You send an email to the team and forget to include the time that an interview candidate is coming in to talk. You want to recall the message before the team reads it, and replace the message with one that includes the interview time.

---

1. Send a message to the recruitment team about **Dexter's Interview**.

   a) Create a new email message.

   b) Address the email message to everyone in the class.

   c) In the **Subject** field, type *Dexter's Interview*

   d) In the message body, type *Dexter will be coming for an interview today.*

   e) Select **Send** to send the message.

2. Recall the message and replace it with a new message that has been fixed.

   a) In the **Folder pane**, select the **Sent Items** folder.

   b) In the message list, open the message you just sent with the subject "Dexter's Interview."

   c) On the ribbon, select **Move→Actions→Recall This Message**.

    d) Select the **Delete unread copies and replace with a new message** radio button.

Recall This Message   ✕

Some recipients may have already read this message.

Message recall can delete or replace copies of this message in recipient Inboxes, if they have not yet read this message.

Are you sure you want to

○ Delete unread copies of this message

◉ **Delete unread copies and replace with a new message**

☑ Tell me if recall succeeds or fails for each recipient

                     [OK]   [Cancel]

---

    e) Verify that **Tell me if recall succeeds or fails for each recipient** is checked.

    f) Select **OK**.
        Your original message about Dexter's interview opens.

    g) In the message body, after the first line of text, type *Dexter will be joining us in Conference Room C at 3 p.m. this afternoon.*

    h) Select **Send**.

    i) Close the original "Dexter's Interview" message.

3. Return to your Inbox and observe the message recall notices.

    a) In the **Folder pane**, select **Inbox** to return to your message list.

    b) Observe the message list.

Student 01   ☑
Message Recall Success: Dexter's Interv...   11:32 AM

If all goes smoothly, you will receive a message with the Subject: **Message Recall Success: Dexter's Interview**. In the message list, the icon reflects the message recall status.

    c) Observe the text of the **Message Recall Success** message.

```
Your message

        To:     Class
        Subject:     Dexter's Interview
        Sent: 10/12/2015 11:32 AM


was recalled successfully on 10/12/2015 11:32
AM.
```

The message content provides basic facts about the recalled message—the recipients, the subject, the recall date and time.

Summary

In this lesson, you used the available options in Outlook for reading and responding to messages. Knowing how to customize your reading options, work with attached files, and use features available in Outlook to manage your responses will help you read and respond to your messages and items more quickly and efficiently.

Do you customize your Reading view in Outlook, or do you use the default views? If you have customized the reading options, how has it helped you organize and manage your emails in your message list?

Do you currently use any of the features or options available in Outlook to help you manage your responses, such as voting, tracking, recalling or resending? What are your experiences with these available features?

> **Note:** Check your CHOICE Course screen for opportunities to interact with your classmates, peers, and the larger CHOICE online community about the topics covered in this course or other topics you are interested in. From the Course screen you can also access available resources for a more continuous learning experience.

5 Organizing Messages

Lesson Time: 45 minutes

Lesson Objectives

In this lesson, you will:

- Manage messages for future action by using categories, flags, and commands.

- Organize messages using folders.

Lesson Introduction

As you start to use Microsoft® Office Outlook® 2016 more and more, the number of messages in your Inbox can become unwieldy. You might need to find emails you have received and quickly respond to them, or you might need to use visible reminders to identify emails that require a response at a later time. By using the features available in Outlook to organize and manage your email, you can be assured that the email needing your attention will be attended to in a timely and professional manner.

TOPIC A

Mark Messages

Once you start using Outlook to send and reply to emails, your Inbox and folders will quickly fill up with messages and items that need your attention. How will you know which messages you need to read, which need you to respond to in order to complete a task, and which you can ignore? You can use the tags, flags, and commands provided in Outlook to help you manage and organize your messages before they clutter your Inbox and derail your productivity.

Mark as Unread/Read

When a message or item arrives in your Inbox, it is indicated as a new message and one that has not been read yet using the blue bar on the left of the message, and blue, bold font for the subject line text. You can use the **Unread/Read** command (found in the **Tags** command group, on the **Home** tab, on the ribbon) to help keep track of the items in your Inbox. Even if you didn't read an item, or read it in the **Reading** pane, you can mark it as read to identify to yourself that it has been handled. Or, oppositely, even if you have already read an email but you want to make sure you come back to the item, you can mark it as unread to give yourself a visual reminder that you need to respond to the item.

Figure 5-1: The Unread/Read command in the Tags command group.

Color Categories

You can categorize your Outlook items using *color categories*, which are color codes that you can customize and assign to items in your Inbox and other folders. You can customize a color category with a specific color and name, and then assign that category to messages, contacts, appointments, and other items to associate them using the category title. Assigning a color category to your items helps you to quickly identify items in your folders and track your interactions with those items.

 Note: To see the color categories that have been applied to items, you must have the **Categories** field displayed in the message list. If it is not displayed, you can display the column by selecting the **View** tab on the ribbon, selecting **Add Columns** in the **Arrangement** command group, and adding the column to your sort bar or moving the field to a location where you can see it. A small box with the color code you selected will display in the **Categories** field for that item.

Color categories can be customized and assigned to items using the **Categorize** command in the **Tags** command on the ribbon.

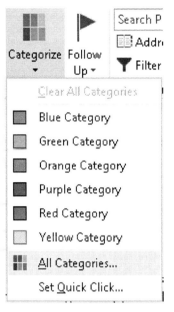

Figure 5-2: The Categorize command allows you to select a color category to assign to your items.

Color Categories and Conversations

A color category that is applied to the top-level message within a conversation thread will be applied to all current and future messages and threads in the conversation. When you attempt to assign a color category to the original item within a conversation thread, Outlook will notify you that this color category will be applied to all items that are part of the selected conversation.

Quick Click for Color Categories

If there is one color category that you frequently use to categorize items in your message list, you can select this color category to be used as your Quick Click for categories. You can select the category using **Categorize→Set Quick Click**. When you select the **Categories** icon for an item in your message list (if the field is displayed in your **Content** pane), the item is tagged with the color code associated with that category.

Shortcut Keys

When you set up a color category, you can also configure a shortcut key to apply to that category. A shortcut key will allow you to use a combination of keystrokes that you configure, such as **Ctrl+F2**, to categorize an email or item with that color category without having to select it from the **Categorize** command group.

> **Note: Outlook on the Web**
>
> You can create and apply color categories to your messages, but if you want to change the categories options, such as the assigned shortcut key, you must use Outlook 2016.

ACTIVITY 5-1
Marking and Categorizing Messages

Scenario

The recruitment effort to hire new employees at Develetech is really picking up. Numerous emails, meeting invites for interviews, and attached résumés are being sent to and from the recruitment team. Your Inbox is starting to become full, and you are having a hard time keeping track of the emails you have received. You want to use tags to help you visually manage the items in your Inbox.

1. Create a custom color category for your emails regarding the recruitment effort.

    a) In the **Content pane**, in the message list, select any email message with the subject line "We're Hiring!"

     Note: When you create a new color category, it is automatically applied to whichever item you have selected in your message list. It is recommended that you first select an email that you want to apply this new color category to before you create the new color category.

    b) On the ribbon, on the **Home** tab, in the **Tags** command group, select **Categorize**.

    c) From the gallery, select **All Categories**.

    ![Categorize menu showing Clear All Categories, Blue Category, Green Category, Orange Category, Purple Category, Red Category, Yellow Category, All Categories..., Set Quick Click...]

    d) In the **Color Categories** dialog box, select **New**.

    e) In the **Add New Category** dialog box, in the **Name** field, type *Recruitment*

f) From the **Color** drop-down list, select the **Dark Orange** color option.

g) From the **Shortcut Key** drop-down list, select **CTRL+F11**.

h) In the **Add New Category** dialog box, select **OK**.

i) In the **Color Categories** dialog box, select **OK**.

j) Verify in the message list that the "We're Hiring!" email now displays a dark orange box in the **Categories** column for the message, and that a dark orange bar titled "Recruitment" displays in the InfoBar in the **Reading pane** of the message.

2. Categorize other emails regarding the recruitment effort with the **Recruitment** color category you created.

a) In the message list, select the email with the subject line "Greg Shannon Info."

b) Select **Home→Tags→Categorize**.

c) From the **Categorize** gallery, select **Recruitment**.

d) In the message list, select any email message with "interview" in the subject line.

 Note: You can use **Ctrl+Click** to select multiple messages at once.

e) On your keyboard, press **Ctrl** and **F11** simultaneously to use the shortcut key to apply the **Recruitment** category to the selected emails.

Flag for Follow Up

Outlook allows you to use follow-up flags to mark certain messages in your folders for follow-up actions. Using the **Follow Up** command in the **Tags** command group on the ribbon, you can mark messages and items and set a reminder to yourself to perform an action on the item at a later date. When you flag a message, the message will display the **Follow up** flag icon.

Note: If the **Tasks** component of the **To-Do Bar** has been enabled, a follow-up reminder for the task will display there as well.

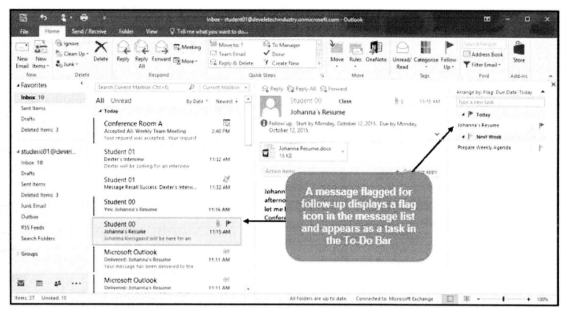

Figure 5-3: A message flagged for follow up.

Follow Up Flag Options

There are a number of options you can choose from when you flag an item for follow up. These options are available when you select an item and select the **Follow Up** command on the ribbon.

Flag Option	Description
Today	Flags the item with a start date and due date of the current day. The default reminder is an hour before the end of workday time established in Outlook.
Tomorrow	Flags the item with a start date and due date of the next day. The default reminder is the start of the following work day.
This Week	Flags the item with a start date of two days from the current day, and a due date no later than the last day of the work week. The default reminder is the start of the work day on the start date (the beginning of the work day two days from the current day).
Next Week	Flags the item with a start date of the first work day of the following week and a due date of the last work day of the following week. The default reminder is the start of the work day of the following week.
No Date	Flags the item without a start date or end date. There is no reminder for this flag.
Custom	Flags the item with a start date and due date of your choosing. You choose what to do as your follow-up action, select a start date and due date, and set up a reminder for the follow-up action.
Add Reminder	Allows you to specify a reminder date and time that is different from the default reminder for the flag type you selected. You can also choose a different reminder sound.
Mark Complete	Marks the flagged item as complete. A completed flagged item is indicated with a **Check Mark** icon in the **Flag Status** field in the message list.
Clear Flag	Removes the follow-up flag and all reminders for this item.

Flag Option	Description
Set Quick Click	Specifies the flag type to be used when single-clicking the **Flag Status** icon for an item in the message list.

Note: Outlook on the Web

Flags work the same way in the online app. If you want to create a custom flag, add a reminder, or use the **Quick Click** feature, you must use Outlook 2016.

ACTIVITY 5-2
Using Flags to Manage Messages

Scenario

After going to the trouble to poll the recruitment team, you want to make sure that you are ready for Johanna's interview. To help you remember, you'll flag the email for follow up and set a reminder to make sure you don't forget.

1. Flag the message about "Joanne's Resume" for follow up.

   a) In the message list, select any of the email messages with the subject line "Johanna's Resume."
   b) Select **Home→Tags→Follow Up**.

   c) From the **Follow Up** list, select **Tomorrow**.

⚑	<u>T</u>oday
⚑	**T<u>o</u>morrow**
⚑	This <u>W</u>eek
⚑	<u>N</u>ext Week

2. Set a **Reminder** for tomorrow at noon.

   a) Select **Home→Tags→Follow Up→Add Reminder**.
   b) In the **Custom** dialog box, verify that the due date is tomorrow and **Reminder** is checked.
   c) From the time drop-down list, select **12:00 PM**.

☑ Reminder		
Wednesday, October 21, 2015 ⌄	12:00 PM ⌄	◀🔊

   You can also change the reminder sound if you wanted to customize it for individual reminders.

   d) Select **OK**.

e) Observe the custom flag and reminder icon in the **Flag Status** column in the message list.

> **Note:** You can right-click the flag icon to display the shortcut menu and change the flag icon, mark it complete, or clear it.

The Ignore Conversation Command

Messages and replies that you receive as part of a message thread can clutter your Inbox. Perhaps you were included on the original message as a recipient, and replies keep coming to you from the other recipients who use the **Reply All** option, even though you don't need to be included on the responses. The **Ignore Conversation** command in Outlook allows you to ignore new messages that you receive as part of a message thread that you no longer want to be a part of. When you use the **Ignore Conversation** command, all messages within the message thread that are currently in your Inbox and any future messages you receive as part of the message thread are automatically moved into the **Deleted Items** folder.

Message threads that you have chosen to ignore using the **Ignore Conversation** command can be recovered and restored to your Inbox from the **Deleted Items** folder.

Figure 5-4: The Ignore Conversation confirmation message.

> **Note: Outlook on the Web**
>
> The **Sweep** feature serves a similar purpose in the online app. When you select the **Sweep** command, you can choose from the following four options:
> - Delete all messages from the selected sender.
> - Delete all, including future messages.
> - Always keep the latest message and delete the rest.
> - Always delete messages older than 10 days.

Clean Up Commands

The **Clean Up** commands help prevent clutter and open up space in your Inbox and other folders by detecting and eliminating redundant messages that are part of message threads. The **Clean Up** commands evaluate the contents of the messages in a thread for redundancy. If the contents of one message are completely contained within another, the previous iterations of that message are cleaned up and moved to the **Deleted Items** folder (by default) or a folder you create.

There are three **Clean Up** commands that can be applied:

- **Clean Up Conversation** evaluates and removes redundant messages only within the message thread of a message that is selected in the message list.
- **Clean Up Folder** evaluates and removes redundant messages from every message thread within the selected folder.
- **Clean Up Folder & Subfolders** evaluates and removes redundant messages from every message thread within the selected folder and any of its subfolders.

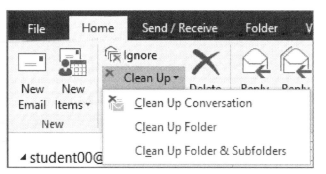

Figure 5-5: The Clean Up commands evaluate and remove redundant messages in your conversations.

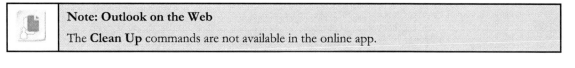

Note: Outlook on the Web

The **Clean Up** commands are not available in the online app.

Access the Checklist tile on your CHOICE Course screen for reference information and job aids on How to Mark and Manage Messages.

ACTIVITY 5-3
Ignoring and Cleaning Up Messages

Scenario

On any given day, you receive many emails in your Inbox. Sometimes, those emails are important and you need to keep track of them, like you did with tags and flags. Other emails aren't as important for you: sometimes you are copied on responses that don't really pertain to you, or emails pile up in your Inbox that are all part of one conversation that could be consolidated. You want to use the **Ignore Conversation** and **Clean Up** commands to help manage your email messages.

---

1. Ignore the email thread from Microsoft Outlook about the delivery receipts, which no longer concern you.

   a) In the message list, select any email message from Microsoft Outlook with the subject line "Delivered: Johanna Resume."

   b) On the ribbon, on the **Home** tab, in the **Delete** command group, select the [Ignore] button.

   c) In the **Ignore Conversation** dialog box, select **Ignore Conversation**.

2. Verify that the ignored conversation was moved to the **Deleted Items** folder.

   a) In the **Folder** pane, select **Deleted Items**.

   b) Verify that the messages with the subject line "Delivered: Johanna Resume" have been moved to the **Deleted Items** folder.

   c) Select one of the ignored messages, and verify that on the **Home→Delete→Ignore** button is now highlighted, indicating that the message has been ignored successfully.

3. Clean up the message thread with "font test" in the subject line.

   a) In the **Folder** pane, select **Inbox**.

   b) In the message list, select any of the messages with the subject line "font test."

   c) Select **Home→Delete→Clean Up→Clean Up Conversation**.

d) In the **Clean Up Conversation** dialog box, review the warning message and select **Clean Up**.

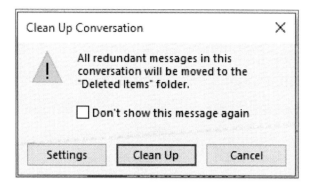

e) Verify that the conversation has been cleaned up and moved to the **Deleted Items** folder.

f) Return to the Inbox.

TOPIC B

Organize Messages Using Folders

In the previous topic, you managed your messages using tags, flags, and other commands in Outlook. It will be even easier to find, interact with, and store messages if you organize them into different and specialized locations. In this topic, you will organize your messages and items using folders.

Using visual prompts and other features in Outlook like tags can help you manage your interactions with the emails in your Inbox. It will be even easier to manage your Outlook items if you keep them organized in folders. In Outlook, you can create and use folders to store messages and items that all relate to one specific subject, such as a project. With folders, you can quickly and easily locate all the items you need to respond to or follow up on in one location

Default Email Folders

Every Outlook 2016 installation includes a number of default email folders that have been created and are available for you to use right away to store your email messages. These default email folders are available for all of your email accounts, if you are accessing more than one account profile through one Outlook instance. These default email folders include:

- Inbox
- Drafts
- Sent Items
- Deleted Items
- Junk Email
- Outbox
- RSS Feeds
- Search Folders

Default email folders in Outlook cannot be moved, renamed, or deleted.

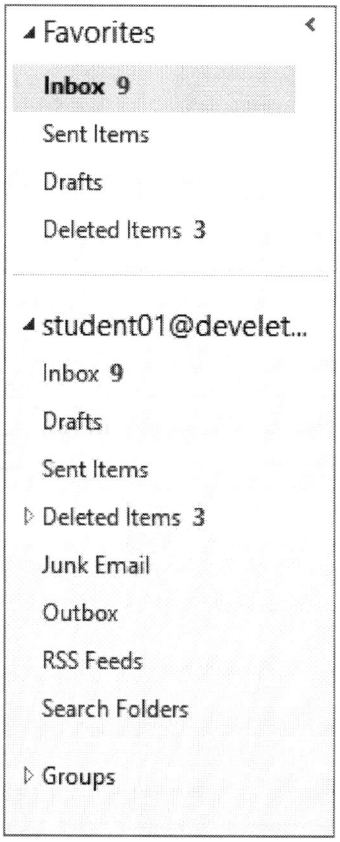

> ◢ Favorites ‹
>
> **Inbox** 9
>
> Sent Items
>
> Drafts
>
> Deleted Items 3
>
> ◢ student01@develet...
>
> Inbox 9
>
> Drafts
>
> Sent Items
>
> ▷ Deleted Items 3
>
> Junk Email
>
> Outbox
>
> RSS Feeds
>
> Search Folders
>
> ▷ Groups

Figure 5-6: The default email folders.

	Note: Outlook on the Web
	In addition to the default folders in Outlook 2016, the online app also includes a **Notes** folder and a **Clutter** folder. The **Notes** folder is specific to the online app and replaces the **Notes** view that appears in the desktop application. The **Clutter** feature can only be activated from within the online app and is covered in more detail in the *Microsoft® Office Outlook® 2016: Part 2* course.

	Note: The default Outlook folder **Sent Items** is also the default location where your sent items are saved, but you can customize where and how your sent items are saved. For more information, check out the LearnTO **Customize Where and How Sent Items Are Saved** presentation from the **LearnTO** tile on the CHOICE Course screen.

Email Folders on the Server

You can create new folders in addition to the default email folders provided in Outlook to help you store and organize your messages. You can use these folders to store and save emails that are all related to a specific subject, such as a project.

Folders you create are saved on the Exchange Server and use storage space that has been allocated for your Inbox. The amount of space allocated is determined by your system administrator.

Folders you create on the server are added to your folder list in the **Folder** pane. Folders you create do not inherit the Reading view or layout that you have customized for your Inbox. You either need to manually customize the reading options and layout for each folder, or use the **Apply Current View to Other Mail Folders** option, found in the **Change View** command on the **View** tab.

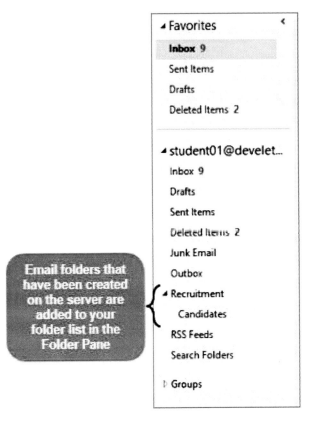

Figure 5-7: Email folders created on the server.

Personal Folders

You can also create *personal folders* in Outlook to organize and store your messages and items, especially those you may want to keep private. Personal folders are saved as Outlook Data files (.pst) and are stored on the local computer. The default directory is **C:\Documents\Outlook Files**. When you are online, the folders are synchronized with the Exchange Server. Because these folders are stored locally, personal folders are available whether or not you are connected to the Exchange Server and they are not included in your allotted network storage space.

 Access the Checklist tile on your CHOICE Course screen for reference information and job aids on How to Organize Messages in Folders.

ACTIVITY 5-4
Organizing Messages in Folders

Scenario

When you start sending and receiving messages in large quantities, your Inbox can quickly become difficult to manage. An easy way to organize and keep track of the messages and items you receive is to create and use folders to store related messages. You want to create a parent "Recruitment" folder where eventually all the information about your recruitment efforts will be stored. Then, you will create a "Candidates" subfolder, where you will store the emails you have received about the potential candidates for the open positions.

1. Create a **Recruitment** folder on the server at the same level as your default folders.
   a) Select **Folder→New→New Folder**.
   b) In the **Name** field, type *Recruitment*
   c) In the **Select where to place this folder** section, select the top level, which is your email account.

Create New Folder	✕
Name:	
Recruitment	
Folder contains:	
Mail and Post Items	⌄
Select where to place the folder:	
⌄ 🔀 student01@develetechindustry.onmicrosoft.cc ∧	
📧 **Inbox** (10)	
📝 Drafts	
📩 Sent Items	
🗑 **Deleted Items** (3)	
> 📅 Calendar	
> 👤 Contacts	
🕐 Journal	

   d) Select **OK**.

e) In the **Folder** pane, verify that the **Recruitment** folder was created, and is now located between the default folders **Outbox** and **RSS Feeds**.

▲ student01@devel...

Inbox **9**

Drafts

Sent Items

Deleted Items **3**

Junk Email

Outbox

Recruitment

RSS Feeds

Search Folders

2. Create a **Candidates** subfolder within the **Recruitment** folder.

a) Select **Folder→New→New Folder**.

b) In the **Name** field, type *Candidates*

c) In the **Select where to place this folder** section, select the **Recruitment** folder.

d) Select **OK**.

e) In the **Folder** pane, verify that the **Candidates** folder was created and is now located as a subfolder within the **Recruitment** folder.

▲ student01@devel...

Inbox **9**

Drafts

Sent Items

Deleted Items **3**

Junk Email

Outbox

▲ Recruitment

Candidates

RSS Feeds

Search Folders

3. Move the messages related to potential candidates to the **Candidates** folder.

a) In the **Folder** pane, select **Inbox**.

b) In the message list, select any email message with **Interview** in the subject line.

c) Select **Home→Move→Move**.
d) From the list of available folders, select **Candidates**.
e) In the message list, select the email message with the subject line "Johanna's Resume."
f) In the **Move** command group, select **Move→Candidates**.
g) In the message list, select and move the message about Greg Shannon with the subject line "New recruit."
h) In the **Folder** pane, select the **Candidates** folder and verify that three messages now appear in the folder.

4. In the **Folder** pane, select **Inbox** to return to your **Inbox** folder.

Summary

In this lesson, you used the available features in Outlook for managing your messages and items. Using color categories and flags provide visual cues, and moving messages into folders keeps your Inbox organized. Additionally, the **Ignore Conversation** and **Clean Up** commands help you maintain a tidy and uncluttered Inbox.

How do you currently manage your email messages? How would you use the options available in Outlook to help you manage your messages?

Do you think that you would use any of the command options that are provided in Outlook? How and why?

 Note: Check your CHOICE Course screen for opportunities to interact with your classmates, peers, and the larger CHOICE online community about the topics covered in this course or other topics you are interested in. From the Course screen you can also access available resources for a more continuous learning experience.

6 Managing Your Contacts

Lesson Time: 45 minutes

Lesson Objectives

In this lesson, you will:

* Create and edit contacts.

* View, search, and print contacts.

Lesson Introduction

As the volume of received mail continues to grow in your Inbox, so does the number of individuals who sent those messages. For the people who you communicate with most often, it would be beneficial to have their contact information readily available. Microsoft® Office Outlook® 2016 provides the Contacts view to manage your contact information. In this lesson, you will create, modify, and manage your contacts.

TOPIC A

Create and Edit Contacts

As you begin to use Outlook more to communicate, you may find that the number of people you interact with has increased exponentially. How do you keep track of everyone? And how do you manage all of their contact information to make those interactions as easy as possible? With the Contacts view in Outlook, you can create and update a list of your contacts quickly and easily. In this topic, you will create and edit contacts.

Contacts

A *contact* is any person with whom you need to communicate for business or personal reasons. Contact information for a person in your Contacts might include his or her name, physical addresses, phone numbers, email addresses, and other information that can help you communicate with that person, such as websites or instant message addresses.

The Contacts View

The **Contacts** view displays your list of contacts in the **Content** pane. The **Home** tab on the ribbon contains buttons and commands for performing contact-related actions, such as creating new contacts, forwarding a contact, and changing the current view. By default, the **Reading** pane is turned on, and the contact information for the selected contact is displayed in this pane.

In the **Reading** pane, you can select **Edit** to modify the details for the selected contact directly in the **Reading** pane. To modify the contact details in the **Contact** window, you can select the Outlook link under **View Source**. In the **Reading** pane, you might see some or all of the following tabs:

- The **CONTACT** tab displays the contact information you have added and saved for that contact.
- The **NOTES** tab displays any notes you have saved in the contact form.
- The **ORGANIZATION** tab displays the contact's organization name. This tab is only available for contacts in your organization.
- The **MEMBERSHIP** tab displays the groups that the contact belongs to. This tab is only available for contacts in your organization.

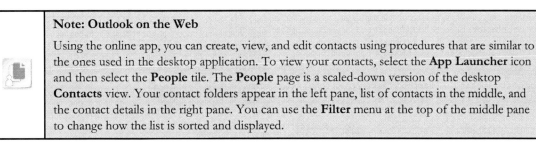

Figure 6-1: The Contacts view.

> **Note: Outlook on the Web**
>
> Using the online app, you can create, view, and edit contacts using procedures that are similar to the ones used in the desktop application. To view your contacts, select the **App Launcher** icon and then select the **People** tile. The **People** page is a scaled-down version of the desktop **Contacts** view. Your contact folders appear in the left pane, list of contacts in the middle, and the contact details in the right pane. You can use the **Filter** menu at the top of the middle pane to change how the list is sorted and displayed.

The Contact Form

Your contacts are created and managed using the contact form. When you select **New Contact** from the **New** command group, a blank contact form opens.

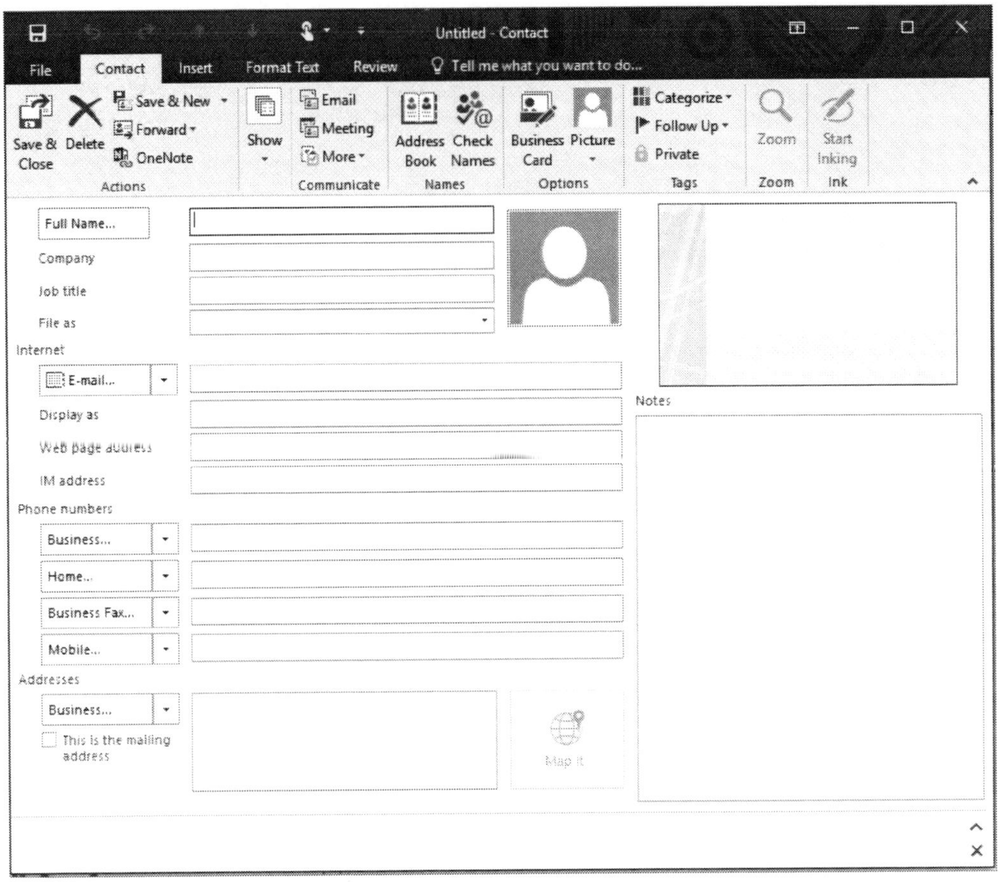

Figure 6-2: A blank contact form.

The contact form has a number of fields where you enter the contact information and details for the person you are creating a contact record for.

Field	Description
Full Name	First and Last names.
Company	Name of the company or organization where the contact works.
Job title	Contact's job title.
File as	How the contact will be filed in the Contacts list. The default setting is "Last name, First name."
Email	The primary email address for communicating with the contact. You can add additional emails by selecting the drop-down list and entering another email address for **Email 2** or **Email 3**.
Display as	How the contact will be displayed when you email them. The default setting is "full name (email address)."
Web page address	The URL of the contact's website, if they have one.
IM address	The Instant Messenger name of the contact, if they have one.
Phone numbers	The contact's business, home, business fax, and mobile phone numbers in their respective fields.
Addresses	The contact's business address. You can add additional addresses, such as their residence, by selecting the drop-down list and entering another address for **Home** or **Other**.

Field	Description
Notes	Additional information pertaining to the contact that might be useful to you.
Contact Picture	A photo of the contact. You can replace the default image icon with an actual photo of the contact. 

The Details Command on the Contact Form

If you need or want to add additional details about your contact, such as a nickname or their assistant's name, you can do so by selecting the **Details** button in the **Show** command group on the **Contact** tab. The available fields are shown in the following figure.

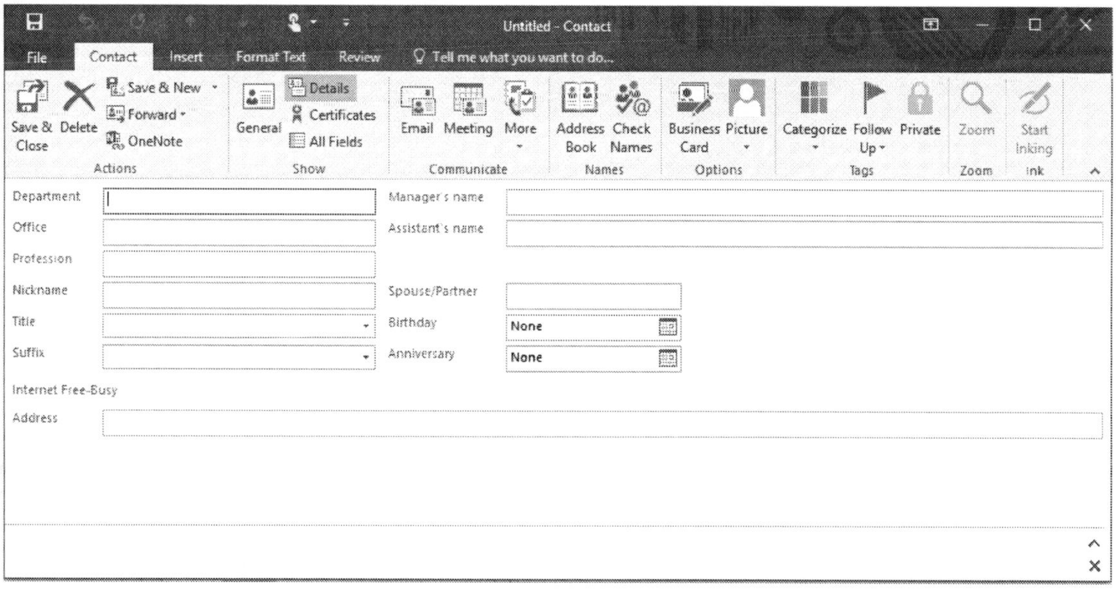

Figure 6-3: The Details section allows you to add additional information about a contact.

Note: Outlook on the Web

When creating a new contact, it is important to select the contact folder first and then create the contact. Moving contacts to another folder is not possible. You can, however, delete the contact and then re-create it in the desired folder.

Secondary Address Books

By default, the contacts you create are stored in the default address book that is created during an installation of Outlook. However, you can create secondary address books in Outlook. *Secondary address books* are additional address books that you can create, name at your discretion, and use to store your contacts. You can create as many secondary address books as you would like to help you organize your contact list.

 Access the Checklist tile on your CHOICE Course screen for reference information and job aids on How to Create and Edit Contacts.

ACTIVITY 6–1
Creating Contacts

Scenario

Develetech is using a global address list in Outlook, so there is always a contacts list of all employees available to you that make communicating with your coworkers very easy. But you also want to manage your own contacts list, where you can keep a robust list of contacts for people you communicate with professionally, including both internal and external contacts. Josh Kincaid is a customer of yours, and you communicate with him often. You want to add Josh as a contact so you can easily communicate with him.

1. Add **Josh Kincaid** as a new contact.

   a) On the **Navigation** bar, select **People**.

   b) Select **Home→New→New Contact**.

   A new contact form opens with the title "Untitled - Contact."

   c) In the **Full Name** field, type *Josh Kincaid* and press **Tab**.
   As soon as you press **Tab** or select another field, the **File as** field is populated with **Kincaid, Josh**.

   d) In the **Company** field, type *Bit by Bit Fitness*

   e) In the **E-mail** field, type *jkincaid@bxbfitness.example* and press **Tab**.
   The **Display as** field is populated with **Josh Kincaid (jkincaid@bxbfitness.example)** which is the default display format of *"Full Name (email address)"*. This is how Josh's name will appear in the **To** address field of an email message.

   f) In the **Phone numbers** section, in the **Business** field, type *(555) 555-1234*

   g) Verify that the business card has automatically populated with all the contact information for Josh.

   Josh Kincaid
   Bit by Bit Fitness

   (555) 555-1234 Work
   jkincaid@bxbfitness.example

h) Select **Save & Close**.

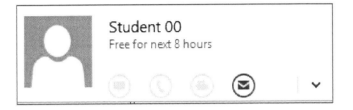

Josh Kincaid now appears in your list of contacts in the **Contacts** view.

2. Create a contact for your instructor (student00@*[your_domain.com]*) from an email message.

   a) On the **Navigation** bar, select **Mail**.
   b) In the message list, select an email message from your instructor.
   c) In the **Reading** pane, in the message content, hover over your instructor's name (Student 00) in the message header until the pop-out for the contact appears.

   ### Student 00
   Free for next 8 hours

   d) On the pop-out, select the **Open Contact Card** down arrow. ⌄

   e) In the **Contact Card**, select the **Add to Outlook Contacts** button. Add
   A Contact Card for your instructor (Student 00) opens with name and email address populated.

   f) Select the **Add Another Field** icon ⊕ next to the **Phone** field, and from the drop-down list, select **Work**.

   g) In the **Work** field, type *(555) 555-6000*

   h) Select **Save**.
   The Contact Card updates to reflect the work phone number.

   i) Close the contact card.

3. Save another student's contact information from an email message by dragging it to contacts.

   a) Observe your contact list and note which student is not listed.
   You will create a contact for one of the missing students.

   b) Switch to **Mail** view.
   c) In the message list, select an email message from the student you just identified.
   d) Drag the message to the **People** icon on the **Navigation** bar.
   e) When the cursor displays a plus sign. drop the message into **People**.
   A new Contact window opens with the selected contact's information, and the selected message content appears in the **Notes** field.
   f) Select **Save & Close**.
   g) Switch to **Contacts** view and verify that the contact has been added.

ACTIVITY 6-2
Editing Contacts

Before You Begin
Contacts provided with the data files were added to your Contacts list.

Scenario
Earlier in the week, one of your coworkers, David, sent an email that included new contact information for your new representative at your corporate travel provider. Rather than creating a new contact, you want to save the attached contact to your contacts list.

- Melinda Joseph, your friend and coworker at Develetech, has recently moved. You want to update her contact information in your contacts list to include her new home phone number.
- George Frome recently retired from Develetech, but you still have him in your contacts list. You want to delete the contact for George.

---

1. Update **Melinda Joseph's** contact information to include her new phone number.
   a) In your contact list, find and select **Melinda Joseph**.
   b) In the **Reading** pane, select **Edit**.
   c) Next to the **Phone** field, select the add another field icon ⊕ and from the drop-down list, select **Home**.
   d) In the **Home** field, type *(555) 555-6280*
   e) Select **Save**.

2. Delete **George Frome** from your contact list.
   a) In your list of contacts, find and select **George Frome**.
   b) Select **Home→Delete→Delete**.

   Unlike most delete actions, you are not prompted to confirm the deletion. You can, however, undo the deletion by using the keyboard shortcut (**Ctrl+Z**) or selecting the **Undo** button in the **Quick Access Toolbar**.
   c) Verify that George Frome no longer appears in your list of contacts.

ACTIVITY 6–3
Creating a Contact Group

Scenario

Because you've been sending the same message to multiple email addresses, it would be helpful and reduce the amount of typing and selecting if you could enter one name that includes the email addresses for everyone.

1. Create a contact group that includes everyone in the class.

   a) Select **Home→New→New Contact Group**.

   b) In the **Name** field, type *Class*
   c) On the **Contact Group** tab, select **Add Members→From Address Book**.
   d) Verify that the **Address Book** field displays **Global Address List**. If not, select it from the drop-down list.

   Select Members: Global Address List

   Search: ◉ Name only ○ More columns   **Address Book**

   [   ] [Go]   [Global Address List – student01@develetechindus ∨]

   e) In the **Select Members: Global Address List** dialog box, select **Student 00** and press and hold **Shift** while selecting the **Student ##**, where ## represents the highest number in class.

   Conference Room B
   Conference Room C
   Student 00
   Student 01
   Student 02
   Student 03
   Student 04
   Student 05

   f) Select the **Members** button.

   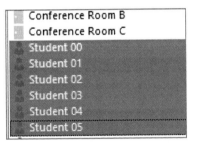

   [Members ->]   Student 00; Student 01; Student 02; Student 03; Student 04; Student 05

   Everyone in the class now appears in the **Members** field.

   g) Select **OK** to close the **Select Members: Global Address List** dialog box.

2. Verify that the **Class** group contains all student email addresses.

Name	Class
📄 Name ▲	
👤 **Student 00**	
👤 Student 01	
👤 Student 02	
👤 Student 03	
👤 Student 04	
👤 Student 05	

3. Select **Save & Close**.

TOPIC B

View and Print Contacts

Once you have added contacts to your Contacts, you will need to be able to view and organize those contacts in an easy and streamlined manner. Knowing how to change the layout of the **Contacts** view enables you to locate and work with the contact information for people you communicate with often. In this topic, you will view, search for, and print contacts.

In addition to the contacts you may have access to as part of a **Global Address List** for your company, the **Contacts** view and the address books you can create for yourself are additional places for you to store and organize the contact information for those people you communicate with frequently. Knowing how to view this information and organize it in an easily accessible manner make it easier for you to manage your contacts.

Electronic Business Cards

An electronic business card is a feature in Outlook that can be used to easily create, view, and share contact information with others. In the contact form, it looks just like a printed business card, and displays any contact information that has been saved for the specific contact. Just like a printed business card, the design of the electronic business card can be customized to include a background, images, or a company logo by selecting **Business Card** on the ribbon.

You can create your own personal electronic business card (or multiple business cards) and share them with your contacts by attaching them to your email messages by selecting **Attach Item→Business Card**. The attached business card will be a file with a .vcf extension. You can also include your electronic business card in your email signature, making it easier for people you communicate with to view and save your contact information.

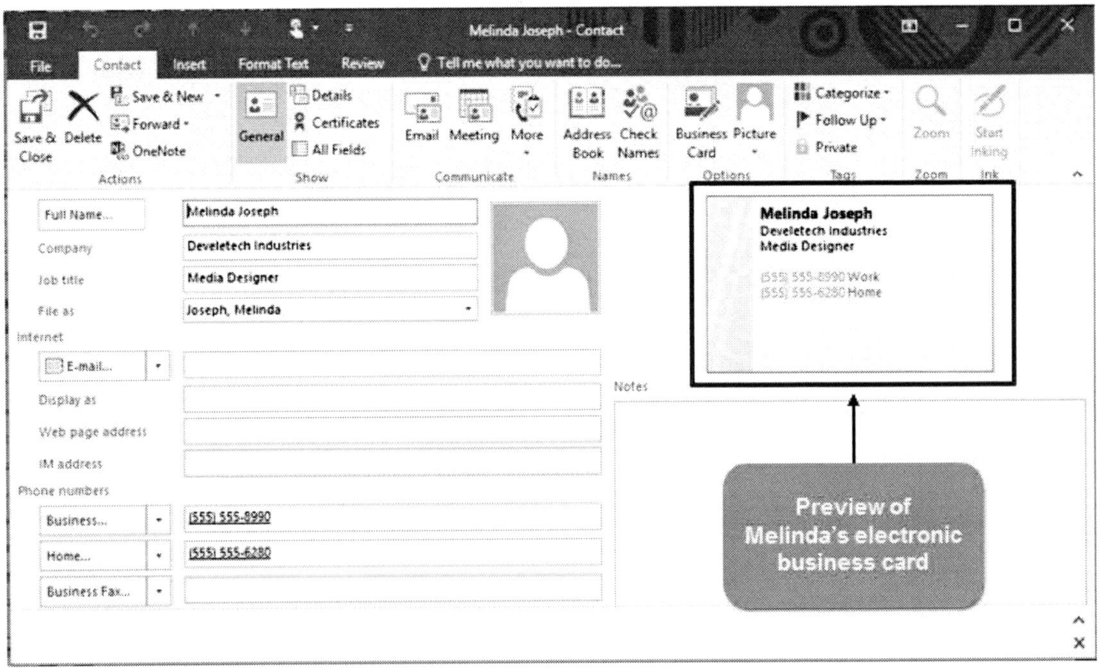

Figure 6–4: Electronic Business Cards.

> **Note: Outlook on the Web**
>
> This feature is not available in the online app. You must use the desktop application to create business cards.

Contact Views

Outlook provides a variety of ways in which you can display the contacts in your contact list. These view options are found on the **Home** tab, in the **Current View** command group.

Figure 6-5: Contact views provide different ways to display your contacts.

- **People** displays your contacts in a list format. In this default view, your contacts are listed in ascending alphabetical order (A to Z) by last name in the **Content** pane, and the contact information for a selected contact is displayed in the **Reading** pane.
- **Business Card** displays each of your contacts as a business card with their contact information, in ascending alphabetical order (A to Z) by last name.
- **Card** displays a small card for each of your contacts, in descending alphabetical order (Z to A) by last name, with the contact information for the contact selected displayed in a **Reading** pane below the contact list.
- **Phone** displays a list of your contacts with business phone numbers as the primary category, in ascending alphabetical order by last name.
- **List** displays a list of your contacts, grouped together by a common category such as a company, with each group in ascending alphabetical order by last name.

> **Note: Outlook on the Web**
>
> You can use the **Filter** menu to change how your contact list is sorted and displayed.

Sort Options

By default, your contacts are sorted in alphabetical order. Depending on the selected **Contact** view, this may be in either ascending or descending order. You can modify the sort options in a number of ways:

- The **Reverse sort** command, found on the **View** tab in the **Arrangement** command group, will reverse the order in which your contacts are sorted. If your contacts are sorted in ascending alphabetical order, using the **Reverse sort** option will list them in descending alphabetical order. This is helpful if you need to quickly find a contact at the opposite end of the sort order.

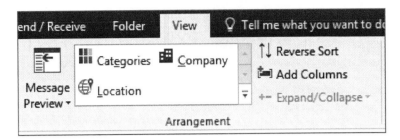

Figure 6-6: The Arrangement command group.

- You can also configure advanced sort settings for the different contact views using the **Sort** options in the **Advanced View Settings** options. To access the **Sort** options, select **View→Current View→View Settings**. In the **Advanced View Settings** dialog box, select **Sort**. In the **Sort** settings, you can configure up to four ways in which to sort your items, and in what manner (ascending versus descending).

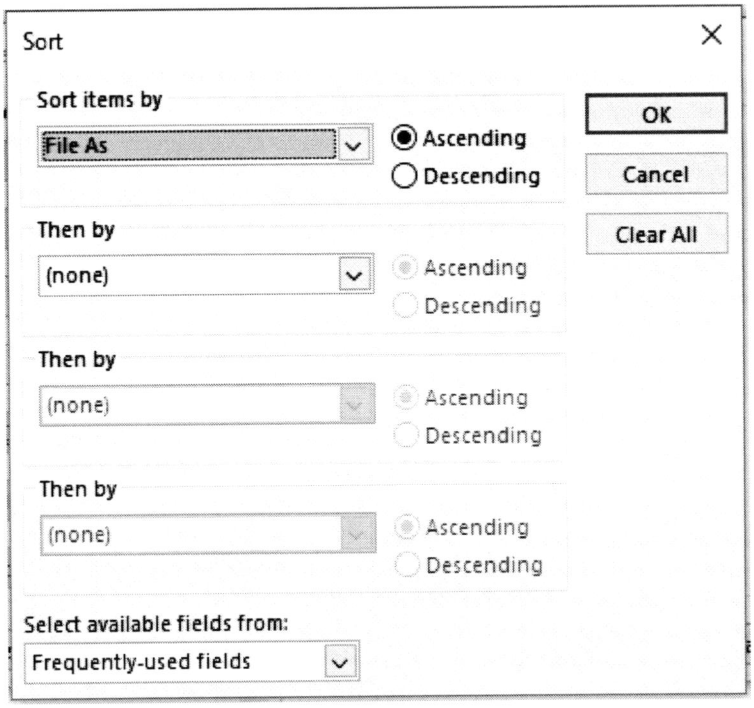

Figure 6-7: The Sort dialog box.

ACTIVITY 6-4
Viewing Contacts

Scenario

As you create and save more contacts into your contact lists, you find that it is becoming more difficult to keep track of all of the people you communicate with. You want to use the different views available in Outlook to display and view your contacts.

1. Explore the different views available for displaying your contacts.

   a) On the **Home** tab, observe the available views in the **Current View** command group.

   You can see the available views for your contacts, and the **People** view is the default view.

   > **Note:** If all of the available views are not visible, you can select the **More** drop-down arrow to expand the list.

   b) From the available views, compare the **Business Card** and the **Card** views.

2. **How are the Business Card and the Card views different?**

3. From the available groups, compare the **Phone** and **List** views.

4. **How are the Phone and List views similar? How are they different?**

5. Using the **People** view, change the sort order of the contact list.

   a) Select the **People** view.
   By default, your contacts are sorted alphabetically by last name and listed in ascending order, from A to Z.

   b) Select the **View** tab.

   c) In the **Arrangement** command group, select the ⇅ Reverse Sort button.
   Your contacts are now sorted alphabetically by last name, but listed in descending order.

   > **Note:** When you apply sort options, only the current view is affected. You will need to specify sort options again if you switch views.

   d) Return to the default A-Z sort order.

6. Change the arrangement of the **List** view.
   a) Select **Home→Current View→List**.
   All of the **Arrangement** commands are available in this view. Notice that the contacts are currently grouped by Company.
   b) Select **View→Arrangement →Categories** to group the contacts by Categories.

   The contacts without a category are grouped together and listed first, followed by contacts in the Recruitment category.
   c) In the **Current View** command group, select **Reset View**.
   d) When prompted to confirm resetting the view, select **Yes**.

7. Display the **Reading** pane to view details for your contacts without having to open the contact.
   a) Select **View→Layout→Reading Pane→Right**.

   The **Reading** pane appears on the right side of the Outlook window.
   b) Select any contact in the contacts list.
   The selected contact's information now appears in the **Reading** pane.
   c) Turn off the **Reading** pane.

The Search Contacts Feature

There are two different ways to search for contacts in Outlook:

- The **Search Contacts** text box located directly above the contacts list.
- The **Search People** text box located on the **Home** tab in the **Find** command group.

Available in the **Contacts** view, the **Search Contacts** text box enables you to search for and find contacts in any of your address books based on selected criteria, such as the first name of a contact, company name, or a phone number. By default, Outlook searches the current folder and displays the contacts that match the contents you entered in the **Search Contacts** box. The **Search Tools→Search** tab contains additional commands that you can use to change the scope of your search, refine your search, and more.

 Note: Outlook stores the keywords you have used. If you have searched for a contact previously using a search term, you can easily repeat the search by selecting **Recent Searches** and then selecting the search term from the list.

The **Search People** text box can be used to search for a contact based on their name, email address, or company name. Outlook will begin searching when you enter a single letter or part of the name. You cannot search for contacts based on phone number, but the **Search People** text box appears on the **Home** tab for all Outlook views—**Mail**, **Calendar**, **Contacts**, **Notes**, and **Tasks**.

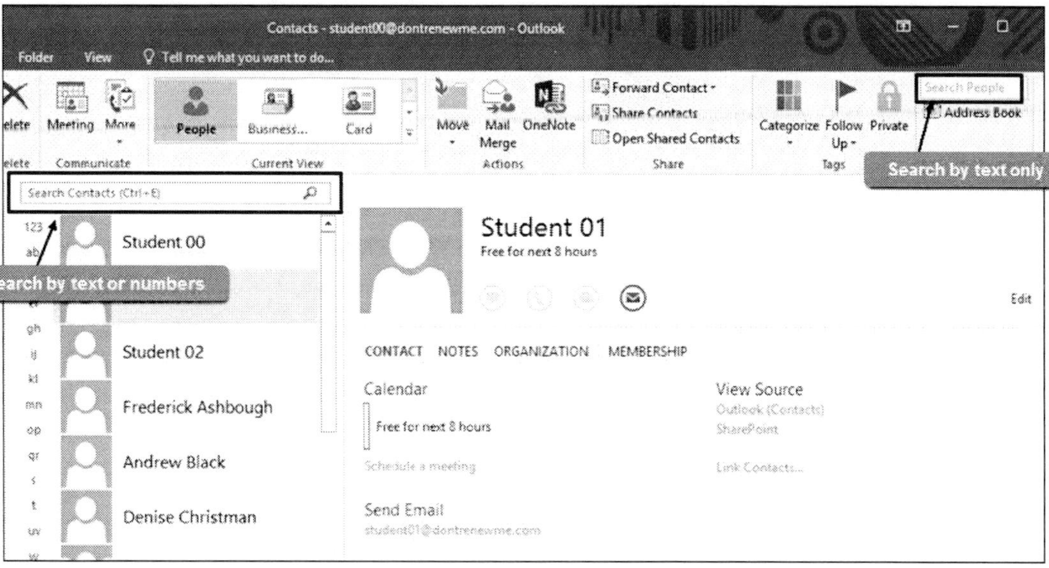

Figure 6–8: Using the Search Contacts text box.

> **Note: Outlook on the Web**
>
> In the online app, the **Search** box appears at the top of the left pane. You can search by text or numbers and further refine the search by selecting a specific folder or directory to search.

People Peek Search

You can also use the **People Peek** in the **Navigation** bar to search for contacts in Outlook. The **Search People** text box that appears at the top of the People Peek functions in the same way as the **Search People** text box on the **Home** tab of every view. You can search based on names and company names, but not other contact information such as address or phone number.

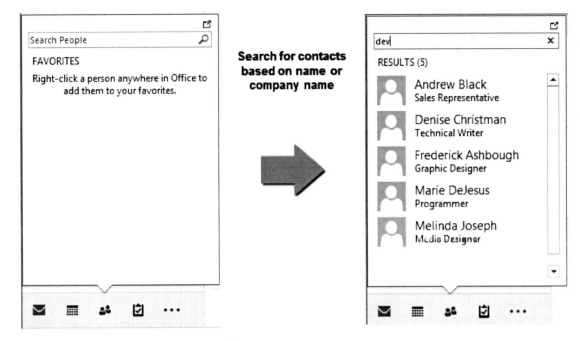

Figure 6-9: Using the People Peek to find contacts.

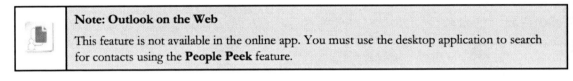

Note: Outlook on the Web

This feature is not available in the online app. You must use the desktop application to search for contacts using the **People Peek** feature.

ACTIVITY 6-5
Searching Contacts

Scenario

You've learned that Brent Haywood has changed jobs and is now working at Develetech Industries so you need to update his contact information. Also, you want to verify that your other Develetech contacts are still relevant.

1. From **People** view, search for **Brent Haywood**.

   a) Select **Home→Current View→People** to display the **People** view.

   b) Select the **Search Contacts** text box and then type *B*

   > Note: You can also press **Ctrl+E** to activate the **Search Contacts** text box.

   c) Observe the search results.
   Outlook begins searching and the four contacts that match your partial search text of "B" appear in the contact list. The contextual **Search Tools→Search** tab now appears with commands and options for refining your search.

   d) Select **Brent Haywood**, and then select **Outlook (Contacts)** to open the full Contact window.

   e) In the **Company** field, type *Develetech Industries*

   f) Select **Save & Close**.

2. Use the **Search Contacts** text box to search for all contacts who work at **Develetech**.

   a) In the **Search Contacts** text box, type *develetech*

b) Observe the search results.

Six contacts match your search text of "develetech" and appear in the contact list.

c) Select each contact and verify that the Company name in the **Reading** pane is **Develetech Industries**.

Print Styles

When printing your contacts, there are a number of styles from which you can choose, ranging from printing the details for a single contact, to printing an entire address book worth of contacts. When you select **File**→**Print** from the **Contacts** view, the print styles are displayed in the **Settings** section, in the **Backstage** view.

Print Style	*Description*
Card Style	Prints an address book of all your contacts, with each contact as a business card with available contact information. Contacts are listed in alphabetical order, but depending on the view selected, they may be listed in either ascending or descending order.
Small Booklet Style	Prints a small-sized booklet of your address book, with each contact and their contact information. Contacts are listed and grouped alphabetically by last name, but depending on the view selected, they may be listed in either ascending or descending order.
Medium Booklet Style	Prints a medium-sized booklet of your address book, with each contact and their contact information. Contacts are listed and grouped alphabetically by last name, but depending on the view selected, they may be listed in either ascending or descending order.
Memo Style	Prints the contact information for a single contact. By default, the first contact in an address book is selected and its information is displayed. To print a specific contact's information, you must first select the contact in the list before accessing the **Print** option.

Print Style	Description
Phone Directory Style	Prints your contacts like a phone book, with only a name and any available telephone numbers for the contact. Contacts are listed and grouped alphabetically by last name, but depending on the view selected, they may be listed in either ascending or descending order.
Table Style	The only available print style when viewing your contact list with either the **Phone** or **List** view. Prints all of your contacts as a table that includes their contact information. The print style matches the view selected.

Note: Outlook on the Web

This feature is not available in the online app. If you want to print your contact list, you must use the desktop application. You can use the web browser's **Print** command, but you only have control over the page settings and not the content being displayed on the page.

Access the Checklist tile on your **CHOICE** Course screen for reference information and job aids on **How to Work with Contacts.**

Access the Checklist tile on your **CHOICE** Course screen for reference information and job aids on **How to Print Contacts.**

ACTIVITY 6-6
Printing Your Contacts

Scenario

After searching for and selecting only those contacts that work at Develetech, you 'd like to print them to have on hand.

1. Select all of the Develetech contacts.
   a) If the previous Develetech search was closed, repeat the search.
   b) In the **Contacts** list, select the six Develetech contacts that resulted from your "dev" search.

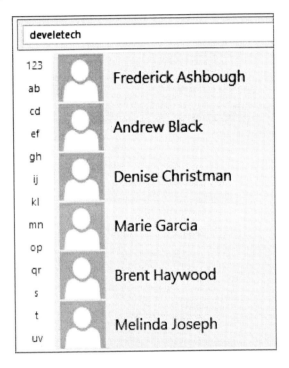

develetech
Frederick Ashbough
Andrew Black
Denise Christman
Marie Garcia
Brent Haywood
Melinda Joseph

You can quickly select all contacts in the list by pressing **Ctrl+A**.

2. Preview how the selected Develetech contacts will look when printed.
   a) On the ribbon, select **File→Print**.
   b) In the **Settings** section, verify that **Card Style** is selected automatically, and observe the preview pane on the right.

    Note: You can zoom in on the print preview if you need to. Your cursor will appear as a magnifying glass when you hover over the preview; select an area of the screen to zoom in on that area.

   The preview shows that all of your contacts will print.
   c) Select the **Print Options** button.
   The **Print** dialog box opens with the same settings that were available on the previous **Backstage Print** page; however, there are some additional options, such as Copies, Page range, and Print range.
   d) Under **Print range**, select **Only selected items**.

e) Select **Preview**.

The preview now displays only the six contacts that you selected in the previous step.

3. Exit **Backstage** view and return to **Contacts**.

Summary

In this lesson, you used **Contacts** view to manage your contacts. Using the Contact features, you created, maintained, and organized the contact information for those people that you communicate or interact with most often. You also experimented with the various ways to sort, search, and print your contacts. When your contacts are up-to-date, well-maintained and well-organized, using the other Outlook features like sending emails or meeting requests becomes even easier.

Do you think you will maintain your own address book of contacts? Will you use contacts more for personal or professional use?

When might you print your contacts? Why might the print feature be useful to you?

 Note: Check your CHOICE Course screen for opportunities to interact with your classmates, peers, and the larger CHOICE online community about the topics covered in this course or other topics you are interested in. From the Course screen you can also access available resources for a more continuous learning experience.

7 | Working with the Calendar

Lesson Time: 1 hour

Lesson Objectives

In this lesson, you will:

- View your calendar.

- Create and manage appointments.

- Schedule meetings.

- Print the calendar.

Lesson Introduction

With Microsoft® Office Outlook® 2016, not only can you use email messages as a form of communication, you can also use the calendar environment to communicate and interact with other users. Using the Calendar feature in Outlook, you can schedule and manage meetings with other people and organization resources, or use appointments to keep track of your own personal events. In this lesson, you will manage your calendar.

TOPIC A

View the Calendar

So far, you have worked with your Outlook Mail and Contacts to manage your email communications. You can also use the **Calendar** view to see the upcoming events you have scheduled. In this topic, you will view the calendar.

Calendar

You can use the Outlook calendar to keep track of your scheduled meetings and personal appointments. As a component of Outlook, the calendar is closely integrated with your mail and contacts so you can incorporate message details and contact information to your calendar events. Depending on how you like to view your calendar, you can choose from a variety of arrangements that provide the amount of detail that you prefer.

Types of Calendar Entries

There are three main types of calendar entries in Outlook: appointments, meetings, and events.

- An *appointment* is an activity that you can schedule at a specific time in your calendar and does not require inviting other people or using other resources such as an online meeting or conference room.
- A *meeting* is an activity which requires inviting other people and possibly requires reserving other resources available in Outlook.
- An *event* is an all-day instance of an appointment or a meeting.

Appointments, meetings, and events can all be scheduled as a one-time instance, or they can be made to repeat multiple times, during the same timeslot, and for a specific purpose. Recurring events are indicated in your calendar with the following recurrence symbol. ↻

| **Note: Outlook on the Web** |
| Using the online app, you can create, view, and edit your Outlook calendar events using procedures that are similar to the ones used in the desktop application. To view your calendar events, select the **App Launcher** icon and then select the **Calendar** tile. The **Calendar** page is a simplified version of the desktop calendar. |

Calendar Grid Arrangement Options

You can choose to arrange and view the calendar grid in any of the different configurations found in the **Arrangement** command group on the **View** tab.

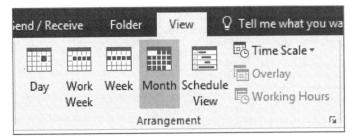

Figure 7-1: The Arrangement commands on the View tab modify the arrangement of the calendar grid.

Options include:

- **Day** displays the schedule of all calendar entries for a specific date, broken down into hourly timeslots.
- **Work Week** displays the five days of a typical work week (Monday through Friday), and the schedule of all calendar entries on those days, broken into hourly timeslots.
- **Week** displays all days in the week (Sunday through Saturday), and the schedule of all calendar entries on those days, broken into hourly timeslots.
- **Month** displays the entire month selected and the schedule of all calendar entries on each day of that month, but does not display the timeslots for each entry.
- **Schedule View** displays a detailed schedule for the current date and time, broken into hourly timeslots for the remainder of the time left in the current day.

Note: Outlook on the Web
There are four different calendar views that you can choose from: **Day, Work Week, Week**, and **Month** views. You can select the desired view from the options in the upper-right corner of the window. Your agenda for the selected day appears along the right side of the window. This is similar to the **Schedule View**, and you can select the double chevrons to hide or show it, as desired.

Time Scale Options

Each hourly timeslot is, by default, divided up into 30-minute segments. Using the **Time Scale** command in the **Arrangement** group, you can select a different increment to divide up each hourly timeslot. The smaller the time scale is in minutes, the more space is available to include details about the specific calendar entry.

Note: The **Time Scale** cannot be modified for the **Month** arrangement option.

The **Time Scale** options include:

- **60 Minutes**
- **30 Minutes**
- **15 Minutes**
- **10 Minutes**
- **6 Minutes**
- **5 Minutes**

Calendar Layout Options

You can customize the layout of the **Calendar** view by modifying which components are displayed and how, including the **Daily Task List**, the **Folder Pane**, the **Reading Pane**, and the **To-Do Bar**. These options can be modified in the **Layout** command group on the **View** tab.

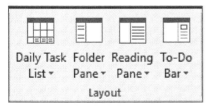

Figure 7–2: Use the Layout commands to customize the Calendar view display.

By default, the **Folder** pane is displayed normally at the left side of the screen, and both the **Reading** pane and the **To-Do Bar** are turned off and do not display.

Note: Outlook on the Web

The calendar layout options and the Daily Task List are not available in the online app.

The Daily Task List

The **Daily Task List** is an optional pane in **Calendar** view that displays the tasks that you have created for yourself or those that have been assigned to you. This task list is off by default, but you can choose to display the task list in Normal or Minimized mode below the calendar grid as shown in the following figure. You must be viewing your calendar in either **Day**, **Work Week**, or **Week** arrangement before you can display the **Daily Task List**.

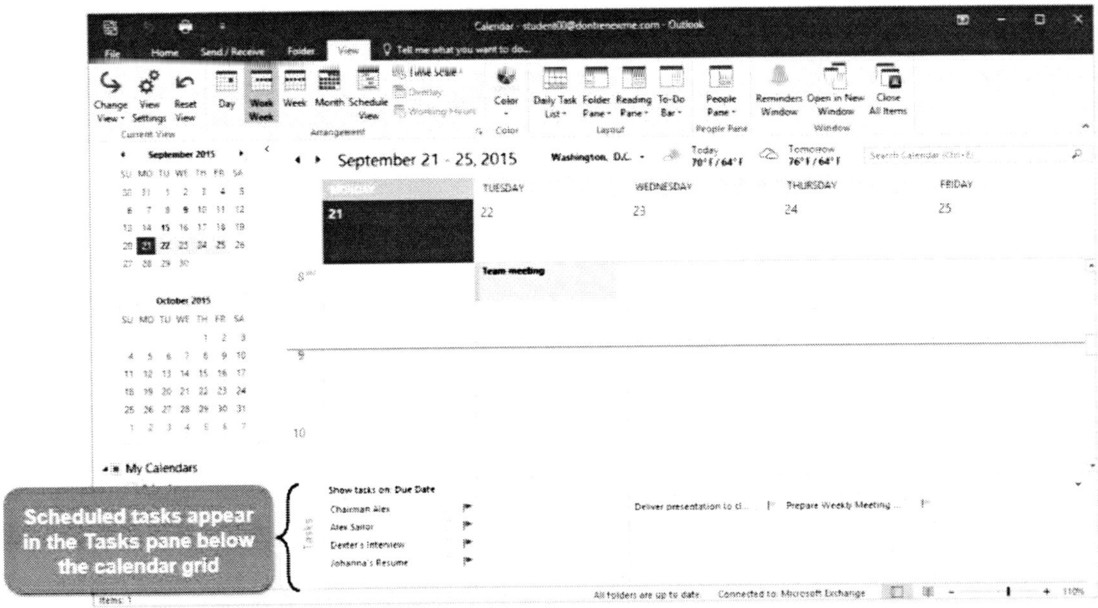

Figure 7-3: The Daily Task List displayed in Normal mode.

Access the Checklist tile on your **CHOICE** Course screen for reference information and job aids on How to Customize Your Calendar Views.

ACTIVITY 7-1
Customizing Your Calendar View

Scenario

Your company, Develetech, recently implemented Outlook as the organization's email client. One of the reasons Outlook was selected was to implement the use of the calendar throughout the organization. You will be using the calendar often to schedule your own personal appointments and meetings, and to keep track of where you and your colleagues are throughout the day. It is important to customize the **Calendar** view in a way that can help you best manipulate and manage your calendar entries.

1. On the **Navigation** bar, select the **Calendar** button.

2. On the **View** tab, in the **Arrangement** command group, explore the different calendar views.

3. In the **Work Week** view, change the **Time Scale** to **15 minutes**.
   a) Select **Work Week**.
   b) From the **Time Scale** drop-down list, select **15 Minutes** to change to 15-minute increments.

   ```
   ⏱ Time Scale ▾

        6̲0 Minutes - Least Space for Details
   ✓    3̲0 Minutes
        1̲5 Minutes
        10 M̲inutes
        6̲ Minutes
        5̲ Minutes - Most Space for Details
        Change Time Z̲one...
   ```

   > **Note:** The **Home** tab also contains buttons to change the arrangement of your calendar; however, the **Time Scale** command is only on the **View** tab.

4. Display the **Daily Task List** in your **Calendar** view.
   a) Observe the **Layout** command group.
   The familiar **Folder Pane**, **Reading Pane**, and **To-Do Bar** buttons are available; however, you now have a **Daily Task List** button for the **Calendar** view.
   b) Select **View→Layout→Daily Task List**.
   By default, the **Tasks** pane is not displayed.
   c) From the list of **Daily Task List** options, select **Normal**.
   The **Tasks** pane appears at the bottom of the screen below the calendar grid in the **Day**, **Work Week**, or **Week** view.

5. Minimize the **Folder** pane.
   a) Observe the **Folder** pane.
   By default, it is displayed on the left side of the screen with the current and next month's calendars displayed at the top, and the list of calendar folders in the bottom portion of the pane.

b) Select **View→Layout→Folder Pane→Minimized**.

c) At the top of the **Folder** pane, select ⟩ to expand the pane.

d) Select 📌 to pin it.

e) Adjust the **Calendar** view to suit your preference.

The Weather Bar

The Weather bar—located at the top of the calendar grid in the **Content** pane, below the ribbon—displays the weather information for the next three days for a selected city. By default, the location that displays in the Weather bar will be the city that corresponds to the market version of Outlook that you have installed, for instance New York, NY.

You can customize the Weather bar to suit your preferences, including selecting whether the Weather bar displays, changing or adding locations, and configuring other options such as whether information is displayed in Fahrenheit or Celsius.

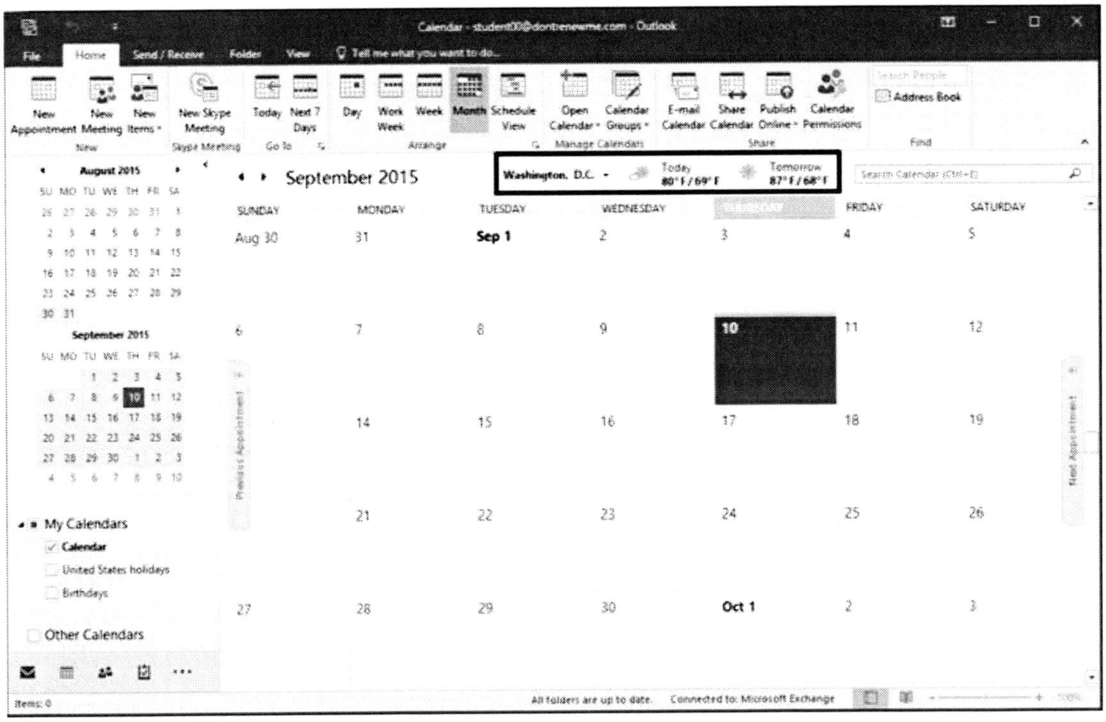

Figure 7-4: The Weather bar displays the weather information for a selected location.

> **Note: Outlook on the Web**
>
> In the online app, a weather icon appears for each day of the current week. The location of the weather icon depends on the calendar view that is selected; however, it is consistently located near the day or date. You can select the weather icon to display a pop-up window with weather details, such as the temperature and a link to the complete forecast at **foreca.com**. If you have multiple locations, you can use the arrows in the upper-right corner of the pop-up window to scroll through the additional locations.

ACTIVITY 7-2
Adding Locations to the Weather Bar

Scenario

You have an upcoming meeting in Denver this week. It would be helpful to know what to pack to avoid getting caught without an umbrella or a proper coat. You can customize the Weather bar to include locations that you will be visiting.

1. Add **Denver, Colorado** to your Weather bar.

   a) View the weather information that appears in the Weather bar for your default location.

Washington, D.C. ▾		Today 70° F / 64° F		Tomorrow 76° F / 64° F

   b) Select the down arrow next to the default location and select **Add Location**.

   Washington, D.C. ▾
   Washington, D.C.
   Add Location

   c) In the search box, type *Denver* and select **Search**.

   Denver   🔍 ✕

   You can select the magnifying glass icon or press **Enter** to initiate the search.

   d) From this list of search results, select **Denver, CO**.

Denver, Colorado ▾		Today 85° F / 57° F		Tomorrow 82° F / 53° F

   The location in the Weather bar changes and now displays the weather information for Denver, Colorado.

2. Add a weather location for your hometown.

   a) Use the **Add Location** command to search for and add a location of your choice.
   You can add up to four additional locations.

b) Toggle between different weather locations.

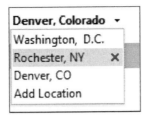

You can select the city name to display the weather location choices. You don't need to precisely select the down arrow.

 Note: To remove a location, select the **Delete** button that appears when you hover over the location in the drop-down list.

TOPIC B

Create Appointments

It is important that you use the calendar in Outlook to keep track of your own individual time during working hours. This includes scheduling and managing your personal events using the Appointments feature. Using appointments, you can keep track of the time that you are unavailable or out of the office, both to help remind you of these personal events and to make your colleagues aware of your availability or whereabouts. In this topic, you'll create and manage appointments.

The Appointment Form

Appointments are created and scheduled in Outlook using the appointment form. You can create a new appointment by selecting **Home→New→New Appointment**.

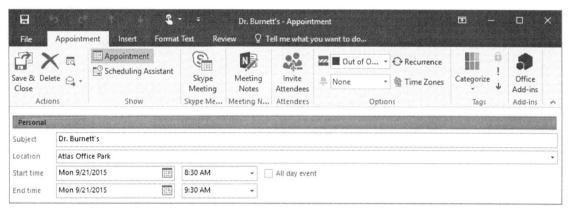

Figure 7–5: A sample appointment.

In the new untitled Appointment, you can enter the details and information about your appointment as follows:

*   In the **Subject** field, enter a brief description or subject matter of the appointment.
*   In the **Location** field, enter the location where the appointment is occurring.
*   In the **Start time** field, select the date when the appointment begins and a start time from the drop-down list.
*   In the **End time** field, select the date when the appointment ends and an end time from the drop-down list.
*   If the appointment is an all day event, with no specific time, check the **All day event** check box.
*   In the message body, you can enter any specific information about the appointment.

> **Note: Outlook on the Web**
>
> In the online app, all three types of calendar entries are created by using the same command of **New→Calendar event**.

Reminders

Reminders are visual and sound alerts that you can set for your calendar entries to notify you in advance of an upcoming event. The default reminder for all-day events is 18 hours prior to the event; the default reminder for events with specific times is 15 minutes prior to the event. You can select different reminder times or choose to have no reminder at all for appointments or meetings you create.

You can schedule a reminder alert by using the **Reminder** drop-down arrow in the **Options** command group of a new event form. You can select the **Sound** option at the bottom of the **Reminder** drop-down list to modify the reminder sound.

Figure 7-6: Setting a reminder.

 Note: Outlook on the Web

In addition to setting a reminder alert with sound, you can also send an email reminder to the attendees or just yourself.

The Show As Options

The **Show As** options, found in the **Options** command group of an appointment or meeting form, can be used to indicate your availability status during a scheduled calendar entry to other people looking at your calendar. Marking your calendar entries with a **Show As** option can help accurately reflect your availability to those looking to schedule meetings with you or to know your whereabouts.

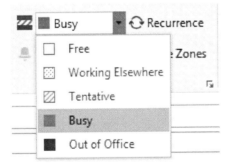

Figure 7-7: The Show As options indicate your availability status.

The show options include:

- **Free** indicates you are available during that time period.
- **Working Elsewhere** indicates that you are working offsite.
- **Tentative** indicates that you may be available during that time period.
- **Busy** indicates that you are busy during the scheduled time period.
- **Out of Office** indicates that you will neither be available nor in the office during the scheduled time period.

 Note: Outlook on the Web

You can specify the **Show As** and **Private** options directly in the new calendar event form.

The Private Option

If you have included information for a personal calendar entry that you want to see as a reminder to yourself, but do not want to make it visible to anyone able to view your calendar, you can mark the entry as **Private**. Calendar entries marked Private will show you as unavailable during the scheduled time but will not show specific details of the appointment, such as the subject or message body. The **Private** option is found in the **Tags** command group on the **Appointment** tab of a new event form.

Private calendar entries are indicated in your own calendar with the lock icon 🔒 displayed in the lower-right corner of the calendar entry.

> **Note:** If you have delegated access rights or have granted read permissions for your calendar to other people, they will be able to view your calendar entries and see the details of your entries, unless you mark them **Private**.

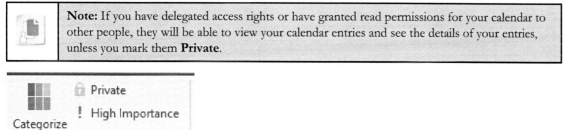

Figure 7–8: The Private command in the Tags command group.

> Access the Checklist tile on your **CHOICE** Course screen for reference information and job aids on **How to Manage Appointments**.

ACTIVITY 7-3
Creating an Appointment

Scenario

Since Develetech will be using the Outlook calendar to keep track of people's availabilities and schedule meetings around those availabilities, it is important that your calendar accurately reflects your day-to-day schedule. You want to schedule and manage appointments for yourself in your calendar to help you keep track of your own personal appointments and to allow your colleagues to view your availability and schedule meetings with you accordingly.

You have a doctor's appointment the following Monday morning at 8:30 A.M., and you want to make a personal appointment for it in your calendar. Since you want to use the appointment to remind yourself as well, you want to make the appointment private so your colleagues can see that you are unavailable, but cannot see the details of the appointment.

1. Create the appointment for your doctor's appointment on your calendar.

   a) On the **Home** tab, select **Work Week** and **Today**.
   Your calendar grid shows only Monday through Friday, and the current day is selected.

   b) Select the **Forward** arrow ▶ to advance to next week.

   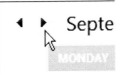

   c) In the **New** command group, select **New Appointment**.

   > **Note:** You can also double-click the 8:30 time slot to create a new appointment for the selected time.

   d) In the blank appointment form, in the **Subject** field, type *Dr. Burnett's*
   e) In the **Location** field, type *Atlas Office Park*
   f) Verify that the **Start time** field displays Monday of next week and modify the time to **8:30 AM**.
   g) In the **End time** drop-down, select **9:30 AM (1 hour)**.

8:30 AM
8:30 AM (0 minutes)
9:00 AM (30 minutes)
9:30 AM (1 hour)
10:00 AM (1.5 hours)
10:30 AM (2 hours)
11:00 AM (2.5 hours)
11:30 AM (3 hours)

h) In the **Options** command group, from the **Show As** drop-down list, select **Out of Office**.

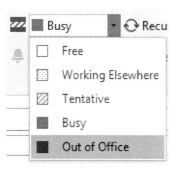

i) From the **Reminder** drop-down list, select **None**.

2. In the **Tags** command group, select [ ] to make the appointment private.

3. Give your doctor's appointment a color category to visually differentiate it on your calendar.

    a) In the **Tags** command group, select **Categorize→Blue category**.
    Because this is the first time you've used the Blue category, you are prompted to rename it.

    b) In the **Rename Category** dialog box, in the **Name** field, type *Personal* and select **Yes**.

    c) Verify that the **Personal** color category appears in the InfoBar, above the subject line, in the appointment form.

4. Select **Save & Close** to save the doctor's appointment to your calendar.

TOPIC C

Schedule Meetings

Now that you have managed appointments in the calendar to keep track of time for your own personal events, you can begin to use the calendar to schedule and manage events that involve your coworkers and your organization's resources. Using the calendar to schedule and manage meetings can help you manage your time and the time you spend with others. In this topic, you will schedule and manage meetings.

The Meeting Scheduling Process

There is a fairly standard process that takes place to schedule meetings in **Calendar** view in Outlook:

1. The meeting organizer sends a meeting request to recipients that have been identified as participants.
2. The meeting is automatically entered on the meeting organizer's calendar when sent.
3. Recipients respond to the meeting request in the manner appropriate to their availability during the meeting time.
4. If accepted, the meeting is automatically entered on each recipient's calendar.
5. A message is sent to the meeting organizer with the response from each recipient.

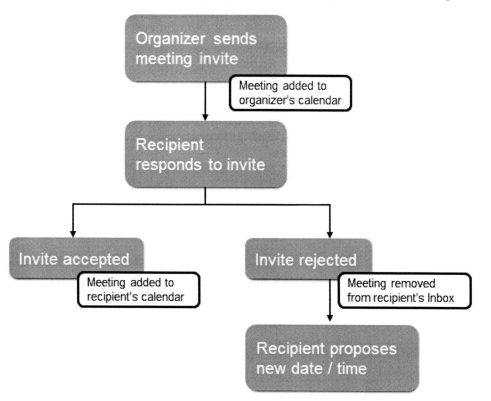

Figure 7-9: The meeting scheduling process.

	Note: Outlook on the Web
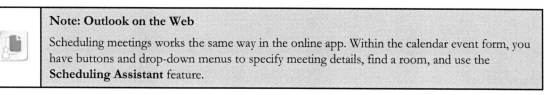	Scheduling meetings works the same way in the online app. Within the calendar event form, you have buttons and drop-down menus to specify meeting details, find a room, and use the **Scheduling Assistant** feature.

The Meeting Form

Meetings are scheduled in Outlook using the meeting form. When you select **New Meeting** from the **New** command group, a blank meeting form opens.

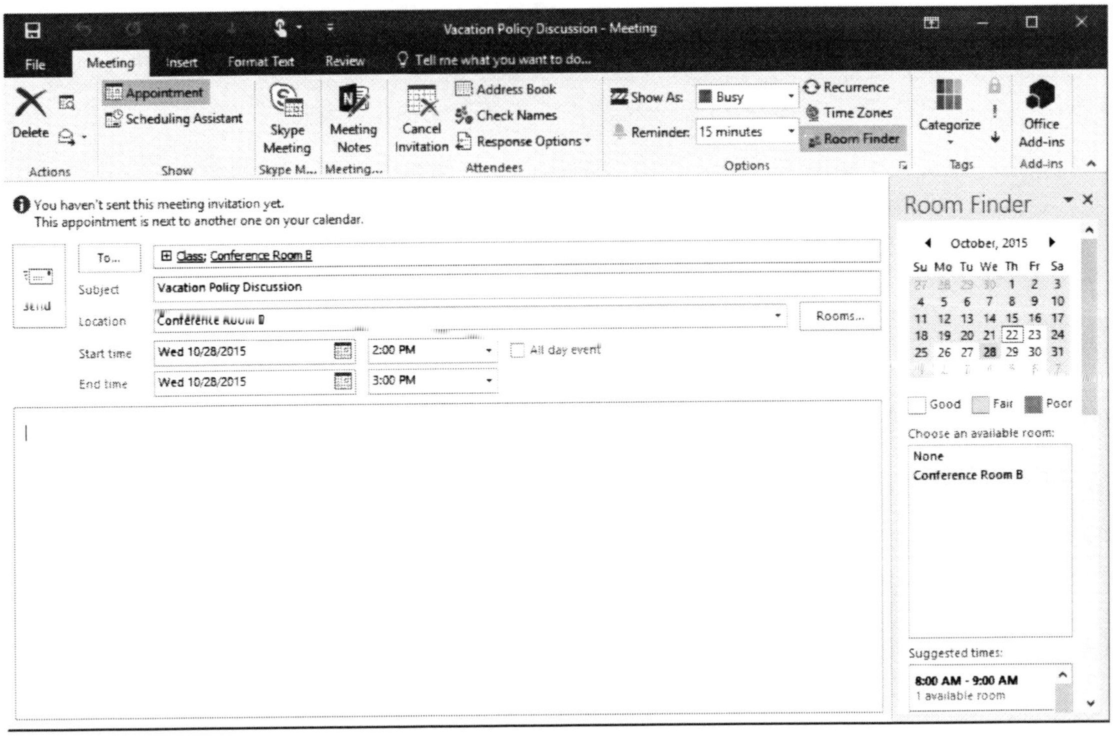

Figure 7-10: Details and options for a meeting are entered into a meeting form.

The meeting form has a number of fields where you enter the details and information about your meeting, select your attendees, and select the necessary options to schedule the meeting.

- In the **To** field, you select your attendees.
- In the **Subject** field, you enter a brief description or subject matter of the meeting.
- In the **Location** field, you can enter the location where the meeting is occurring or select **Rooms** to find and select a room that has been designated as a shared resource for the organization, such as a conference room.
- If the appointment is an all-day event, with no specific time, check the **All day event** check box.
- In the **Start time** field, you select the date when the meeting begins from the calendar and a start time from the drop-down list.
- In the **End time** field, you select the date when the meeting ends from the calendar and an end time from the drop-down list.
- In the message body, you can enter any specific information about the appointment.

Meeting Reminders

You can also set reminders for meetings. The meeting organizer sets the reminder for the meeting when they send the meeting request, but it can be changed by the recipients to suit their own personal preferences once they have accepted the invite. The default reminder for new meetings is 10 minutes prior to the event.

Resource Booking Attendant

The **Resource Booking Attendant** automates the process of accepting or declining meeting requests regarding shared resources, like conference rooms. This feature works by setting policies for automating the meeting response. Policies can be set to book each individual resource.

> **Note:** While you will typically follow the process of using the **New Appointment** or **New Meeting** commands to schedule new events, you can also do so directly from an email message. For more information, check out the LearnTO **Schedule an Appointment or Meeting from an Email Message** presentation from the **LearnTO** tile on the CHOICE Course screen.

The Room Finder Pane

The **Room Finder** pane helps you select the best time and location for your meeting. Based on the recipients, the date, and the time that you have selected in the meeting form for your meeting, the **Room Finder** pane displays important information about the availability of these resources:

- At the top of the pane is a calendar, which displays the date you have selected.
- Below the calendar, the **Choose an available room** section displays the rooms that are available during the time frame you have selected on the date you have selected.
- At the bottom of the pane, the **Suggested times** section displays any conflicts that may occur for any of the intended attendees for the date and time selected. It also suggests times for your meeting when most, if not all, of your attendees are available.

> **Note:** You can find and select a conference room that has been set up in Exchange as a shared resource in the Global Address List, which is the default address book where you select participants. Rooms appear in the Global Address List with a door symbol. Your organization may also set up a separate address book that only includes the shared resources for you to easily find and select.

If the **Room Finder** pane does not appear in your meeting form, then you can select the **Room Finder** button in the **Options** command group on the **Meeting** tab.

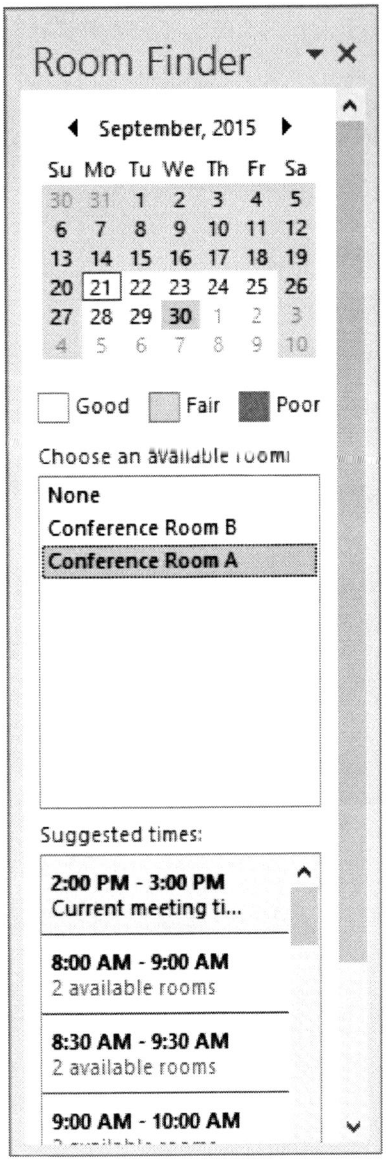

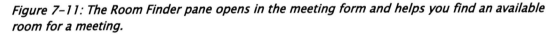

Figure 7-11: The Room Finder pane opens in the meeting form and helps you find an available room for a meeting.

The Scheduling Assistant

The **Scheduling Assistant** is another tool available in a meeting form that helps you identify the availability of participants and resources you are including on a meeting request. On the **Meeting** tab, you can select the **Scheduling Assistant** in the **Show** command group. Once you have added the date, time, and required attendees and resources to your meeting form, you can open the **Scheduling Assistant** to view any possible conflicts for the meeting time, view your attendees availabilities for other time frames, and select the best time for the meeting.

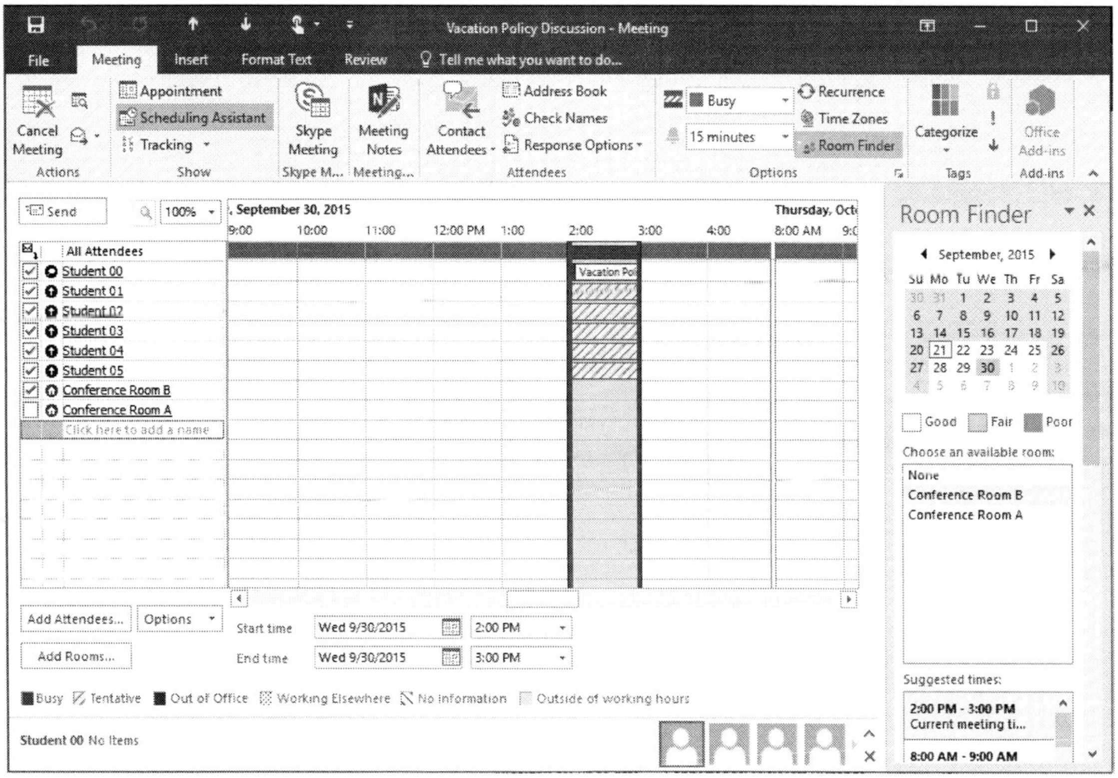

Figure 7-12: The Scheduling Assistant helps you identify the availability of your participants and resources for a specific meeting request.

> **Note:** When you open the **Scheduling Assistant**, the **Room Finder** pane is automatically opened as well.

Toggle Between Meeting Form Views Using the Show Commands

You can toggle between the **Appointment** and **Scheduling Assistant** commands, found in the **Show** command group on the **Meeting** tab, to change the view of the meeting form. If you have opened the **Scheduling Assistant**, you can return to the message form to continue to add information to the meeting request by selecting **Appointment**.

Recurring Meetings

Once you have scheduled a meeting, you can use the **Recurrence** setting to configure the meeting so that it will occur on a regularly scheduled basis. The advantage of the **Recurrence** setting is that you only need to create the meeting once and Outlook will automatically send out the future meeting invitations based on the specified recurrence options.

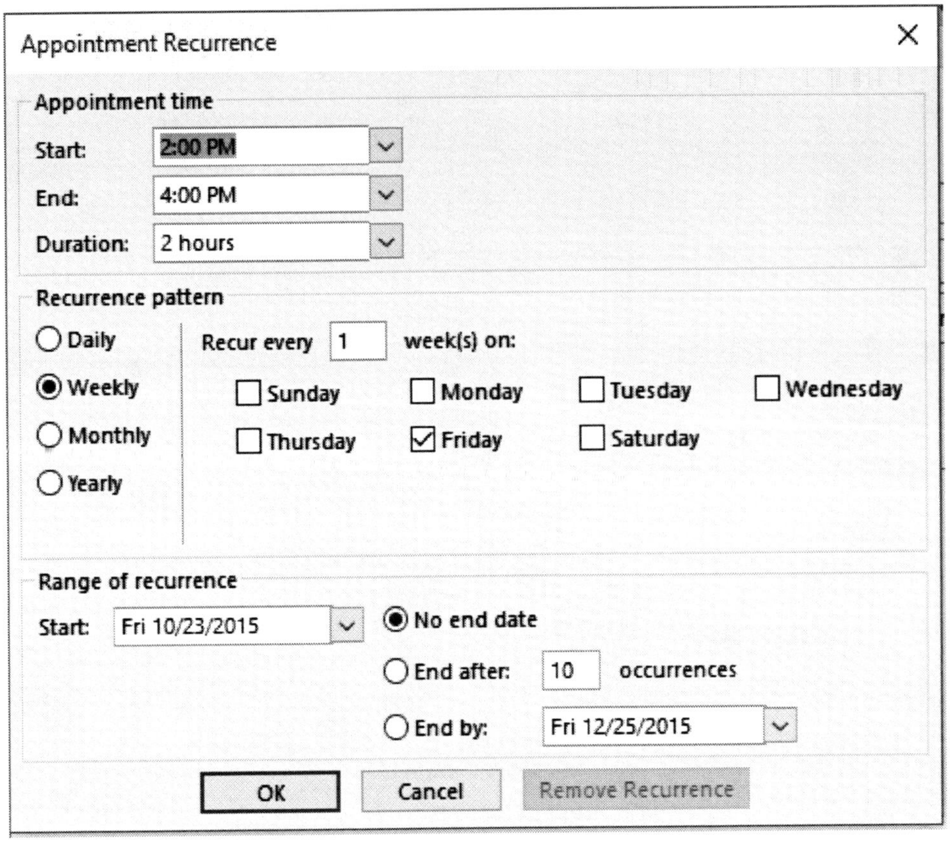

Figure 7-13: The Appointment Recurrence dialog box.

Access the Checklist tile on your CHOICE Course screen for reference information and job aids on How to Manage Meetings.

ACTIVITY 7–4
Creating New Meeting Requests

Before You Begin
You have a contact group named Class.

Scenario
You have been asked to schedule a meeting to discuss the new company vacation policy. Your first choice for the meeting is next Wednesday from 2:00 to 3:00 P.M. To begin with, you'd like to invite everyone to attend, and then, if schedules conflict too much, you might offer an alternative meeting time.

---

1. Create a new meeting with the **Subject** of **Vacation Policy Discussion** for next **Wednesday** at **2:00 PM**.
   a) On the **Home** tab, select **New→New Meeting**.

   b) In the **Subject** field, enter *Vacation Policy Discussion*
   c) In the **Start time** field, select next **Wednesday** at **[*n*]:00 PM** where *n* is the same as your student number.
   d) In the **End time** field, select an end time that creates a one-hour meeting.

2. Use the **Rooms** button to select **Conference Room B** as the location.
   a) At the right end of the **Location** field, select **Rooms**.
   b) In the **Select Rooms: All Rooms** dialog box, select **Conference Room B**.
   c) Select **Rooms** to add Conference Room B to the meeting invitation.

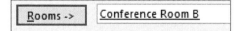

   d) Select **OK** to return to your meeting invitation.

3. Use the **Scheduling Assistant** to make sure that everyone, including the room, is available to attend your meeting.
   a) In the **To** field, type a semicolon and then type *Class*
      You created this contact group in a previous lesson.
   b) Observe the InfoBar.

> ⓘ You haven't sent this meeting invitation yet.
>
> | To... | Conference Room B; ⊞ **Class** |

The InfoBar indicates that you haven't sent the meeting invitation yet.

---

c) On the **Meeting** tab, select **Show→Scheduling Assistant**.

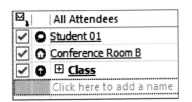

The contact group, Class, is listed as a single attendee. To see the individual student's schedule, you'll need to expand the Class group.

d) In the attendee's list, expand **Class** by selecting the plus sign.

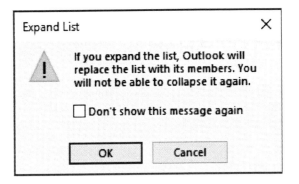

e) Select **OK** to close the **Expand List** message box and replace the group name with the individual members.

☒	All Attendees
✓ ✪	Student 01
✓ ⬡	Conference Room B
✓ ⬆	Admin 00
✓ ⬆	Student 00
✓ ⬆	Student 02
✓ ⬆	Student 03
✓ ⬆	Student 04
	Click here to add a name

f) Observe the legend at the bottom of the **Scheduling Assistant** window.

These indicators inform you of an attendee's availability.

g) Looking at the **Scheduling Assistant** information, verify that your selected time is conflict free for the invited attendees, including the conference room.

h) Select the [📧 Send] button.

4. Create a second meeting invitation:
   - To: *Class*
   - Subject: *Meet to Discuss Candidates*
   - Location: *[your_name] Office*
   - Start time: **tomorrow** at *[n]*:00 where *n* matches your student number
   - Duration: **one hour**

5. Make the "Meet to Discuss Candidates" meeting a recurring meeting for the next **five** weeks.

a) On the **Meeting** tab, in the **Options** command group, select the [⟳ Recurrence] button.

b) In the **Recurrence pattern** section, verify that **Weekly** and the correct date of the week is selected.

c) In the **Range of recurrence** section, select the **End after** radio button and change the number of occurrences to **5**.

```
┌─────────────────────────────────────────────────────────────────────┐
│  Range of recurrence                                                  │
│                                                                       │
│  Start:  │ Fri 10/16/2015    │ ∨ │   ○ No end date                    │
│                                                                       │
│                                  ◉ End after:  │ 5 │   occurrences     │
│                                                                       │
│                                  ○ End by:   │ Fri 12/18/2015 │ ∨ │    │
│                                                                       │
└─────────────────────────────────────────────────────────────────────┘
```

d) Select **OK**.

e) Select the [📧 Send] button.

6. Send a third meeting invitation:

   • To: *Class*
   • Subject: *Lunch*
   • Location: *Ray's Diner*
   • Start time: day of your choice at **noon**
   • End time: duration of your choice

Share Meeting Notes Using OneNote

One of the most common things that participants in a meeting actually do during the meeting is take notes. Outlook 2016 integrates seamlessly with OneNote® to help you easily share the notes you have taken during a meeting with the other meeting attendees. You can share your notes using OneNote before your meeting by integrating a link with OneNote in the meeting request, or during a meeting by sharing your OneNote document with the meeting attendees.

When meeting notes are shared using OneNote, a link to the OneNote document is placed in the meeting request, and the meeting information is placed in the linked OneNote document.

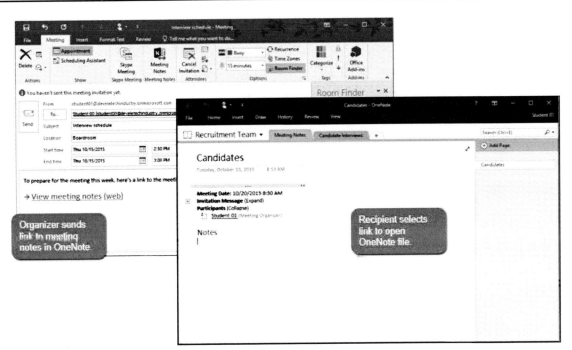

Figure 7-14: Sharing meeting notes with OneNote.

> **Note: Outlook on the Web**
>
> Incorporating OneNote meeting notes into an Outlook meeting is not available when using Outlook on the web. However, you can share your OneNote notes with others by sharing from within OneNote directly and not through Outlook.

> **Access the Checklist tile on your CHOICE Course screen for reference information and job aids on How to Share Meeting Notes Using OneNote.**

Meeting Response Options

When you receive a meeting invitation, you can respond inline in the **Reading** pane, or open the invitation in a separate window. There are a number of response options available for responding to a meeting request.

Response Option	Description
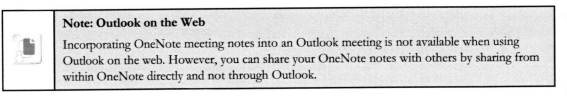 ✓ Accept ▼	Use **Accept** to accept the meeting invitation and place the meeting on your calendar. You can choose to accept and send a response to the meeting organizer, accept and not send a response to the meeting organizer, or accept and edit the response to include information in a message to the meeting organizer.
? Tentative ▼	Use **Tentative** to tentatively accept the meeting invitation and place the meeting on your calendar showing as Tentative. You can choose to tentatively accept and send a response to the meeting organizer, tentatively accept and not send a response to the meeting organizer, or tentatively accept and edit the response to include information in a message to the meeting organizer. The **Tentative** response would most likely be used in situations when you are not a required attendee or to indicate that you may be able to attend the meeting.

Response Option	Description
✕ Decline ▾	Use **Decline** to decline the meeting invitation. You can choose to decline and send a response to the meeting organizer, decline and not send a response to the meeting organizer, or decline and edit the response to include information in a message to the meeting organizer.
Propose New Time ▾	Use **Propose New Time** if you cannot attend the meeting at the time scheduled. You can either tentatively accept the meeting and propose a new time, or decline the meeting and propose a new time. If you do not choose either option (**Tentative** or **Decline**), and simply choose **Propose New Time**, by default you tentatively accept the meeting. The meeting is placed on your calendar at the time you proposed until the meeting organizer accepts or rejects your proposed time.
Respond	The **Respond** command provides a number of other response options that do not pertain to the meeting invite. When you choose one of these response options, the meeting request is not accepted or declined. You can choose to respond to the sender in a different manner before replying to the meeting request. The available options are: **Reply**, **Reply All**, **Forward**, or **Forward as Attachment**.

Note: Outlook on the Web

When responding to meeting invitations, you have three response options: **Accept**, **Tentative**, and **Decline**. Unlike in the desktop application, you do not have the opportunity to add comments to your responses or propose a new time.

Note: You know how to update information for a meeting, but what if that update or reschedule only applies to one instance in a recurring meeting? For more information, check out the LearnTO **Reschedule One Meeting in a Recurring Meeting Series** presentation from the **LearnTO** tile on the CHOICE Course screen.

ACTIVITY 7-5
Accepting and Declining Meeting Requests

Scenario

Now that Develetech has implemented Outlook as its email client, more people are beginning to schedule meetings through the calendar. There are a number of meeting invites in your Inbox that you need to respond to. You'll accept the lunch invitation immediately. For the Vacation Policy Discussion meeting, you need to decline the meeting due to your travel schedule.

1. Accept the **Lunch** meeting invitation.
   a) On the **Navigation** bar, select **Mail**.
   b) In the message list, select the meeting request with the subject **Lunch**.
   c) In the **Reading** pane, select **Accept** and choose **Send the Response Now**.

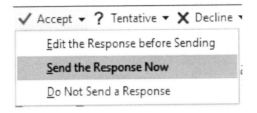

As the invitee, the accepted meeting invitation item has been moved from your message list and added to your calendar. As the meeting organizer, the meeting remains in your calendar and you are notified by email that the invitee has accepted.

2. Decline the **Vacation Policy Discussion** meeting invitation and add the reason for your absence.
   a) In the message list, select the meeting request with the subject **Vacation Policy Discussion**.
   b) In the **Reading** pane, select **Decline** and select **Edit the Response before Sending**.

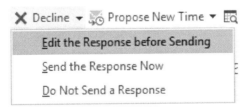

   c) In the meeting invitation window, type a reason for your absence, such as *I'll be out of town.*

d) Observe the InfoBar and Subject of the meeting invitation window.

> ℹ No, I will not attend.
>
> | Send | To... | Student 00 |
> |---|---|---|
> | | Cc... | |
> | | Subject | Declined: Vacation Policy Discussion |
> | | When | Tuesday, October 27, 2015 1:00 PM-1:30 PM |
> | | Location | Conference Room B |
>
> I'll be out of town.|

Both the InfoBar and the **Subject** line indicate that you are declining the meeting.

e) Select **Send**.
As the invitee, the meeting invitation item has been removed from your message list and your calendar. As the meeting organizer, the meeting remains in your calendar and you are notified by email that the invitee has declined.

3. In your calendar, verify that the **Lunch** meeting has been added and the **Vacation Policy Discussion** has been removed from the calendars of those who declined the meeting.

a) Switch to your **Calendar** view.

b) As the meeting invitee, verify that the **Lunch** meeting appears in your calendar while the **Vacation Policy Discussion** meeting does not.

 Note: If necessary, you can double-check the date and time of the meeting invitation by opening the **Declined** response in your **Sent Items** folder.

c) As the meeting organizer, verify that both meetings appear on your calendar.

ACTIVITY 7-6
Proposing a New Time for a Meeting

Scenario

Unfortunately, you have a meeting with the Director of Finance on the same day that your Recruitment team leader wants to talk about the candidates. Both meetings are important, so you would like to propose a new time for the meeting to occur. Because your attendance is important at both meetings, the team leader will accommodate you by changing the meeting time.

1. As the meeting attendee, decline the **Meet to Discuss Candidates** meeting and propose a new time.

   a) In Mail, select your **Inbox** folder, if it's not already displayed.

   b) In the message list, select the meeting request with the Subject **Meet to Discuss Candidates** from the student one number higher than you.

   c) In the **Reading** pane, select **Propose New Time→Decline and Propose New Time**.

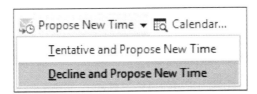

2. Propose a new meeting time and verify that the other attendees are still available.

   a) In the **Propose New Time: Meet to Discuss Candidates** dialog box, in the **Meeting start time** field, select **10:00 AM**.

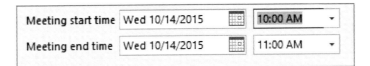

b) In the **Propose New Time** dialog box, verify that the attendees are free and available to meet during the time you selected.

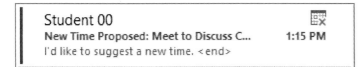

c) Select **Propose Time**.
    A new message window opens for you to enter text in the message body.

d) Observe the name in the **To** field.
    By default, the new proposed time is sent to only the meeting organizer. This gives the organizer an opportunity to accept the proposed time or counter with a different time before the meeting is updated on all attendees' calendars.

e) In the message body, type a message of your choice.

f) Select **Send**.
    The meeting invitation has been removed from your message list.

3. As the meeting organizer, view and accept the newly proposed meeting time.

a) As the meeting organizer, select the **New Time Proposed** email that you've received.

Student 00
New Time Proposed: Meet to Discuss C...   1:15 PM
I'd like to suggest a new time. <end>

b) Double-click the proposal email to open the meeting proposal in a separate window.

c) On the **Meeting Response** tab, select **Accept Proposal**.
Your original meeting invitation opens with the new time you just accepted.

d) Select **Send Update** to update the meeting on the attendees' calendars.
As the organizer, the meeting has been updated in your calendar.

4. As the meeting attendee, accept the updated **Meet to Discuss Candidates** invitation.

TOPIC D

Print the Calendar

Now that you have scheduled both appointments and meetings in your calendar, your calendar should be a good representation of when you are free and when you are busy. There might be times when you want to print your calendar or calendar entries to have a hard copy of the information, rather than having to access Outlook to see it. In this topic, you will print your calendar.

Calendar Print Styles

When you select **File→Print** from the **Calendar** view, the print styles are displayed in the **Settings** section in the **Backstage** view.

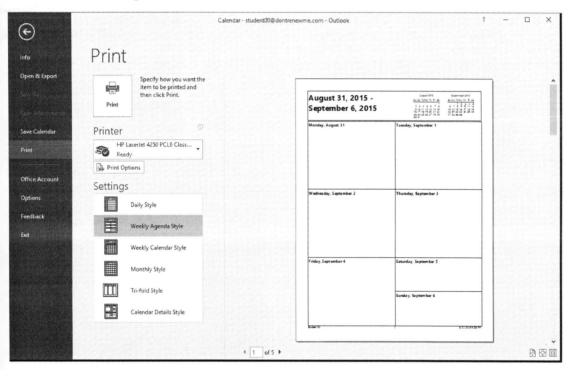

Figure 7–15: Printing the calendar.

When printing your calendar, there are a number of styles from which you can choose, ranging from printing the details for a single event, to printing the details for all events in a single month. The following table defines the available print styles.

Print Style	Description
Memo Style	Available only when a calendar event is selected or opened. It prints the details of the specific event.
Daily Style	Prints the events for a single day, broken down by hourly time slots. Also includes the **Daily Task List** and any available **Notes** for the day.
Weekly Agenda Styles	Prints the events for the entire week (Monday through Sunday), in the form of a daily agenda. Each day of the week has its own slot, with that day's events listed with their times, locations, and other details.

Print Style	Description
Weekly Calendar Style	Prints the events for the entire week (Monday through Sunday), in the form of calendar entries with hourly time slots. Each day of the week has its own set of time slots, with the events of the day listed in the appropriate time slot with location, attendees, and other details.
Monthly Style	Prints the events for the entire month. Events are listed in their appropriate day of the month, with important details for the events like times and locations.
Tri-fold Style	Prints a three-paneled view of events for both a single day and week. The first panel is the events for a single day in the **Daily Style**. The second panel is the **Daily Task** list for that day. The third panel is the weekly agenda for the week in which the selected day falls in the **Weekly Agenda Style**.
Calendar Details Style	Prints the details for all events scheduled in the calendar in a daily agenda style. Whenever there is an event on the calendar, that day and the events that occur on that day—with their important details included—are printed.

Note: Outlook on the Web

When you print your Outlook calendar from the online app, you can choose the type of view, the layout, and the begin and end times that you want to print. You also have the option to print a detailed agenda with the calendar.

Access the Checklist tile on your CHOICE Course screen for reference information and job aids on How to Print Your Calendar.

ACTIVITY 7-7
Printing Your Calendar

Scenario

To help everyone at Develetech keep better track of their colleagues' availabilities and to know where people are to get in touch with them, senior management has asked that each employee print and display their calendar outside their office. You need to print your calendar for the work week.

1. Print your calendar events for the current week in the **Weekly Agenda Style**.
   a) In your **Calendar** view, select **Home→Arrange→Month**.
   b) On the ribbon, select **File→Print**.
   c) In the **Settings** section, select **Weekly Agenda Style**.

   A preview of how your printed agenda is displayed on the right side of the **Print** page.
   d) Use the **Next Page** buttons to scroll through the preview.

2. Modify the print range to print only the current week.
   a) Select **Print Options** to open the **Print** dialog box.
   b) In the **Print range** section, modify the **Start** and **End** dates to be Monday and Friday, of the current week.

   c) Select **Preview**.

d) Select the **Back** button to bypass printing and return to **Calendar** view.

Summary

In this lesson, you used the Calendar feature in Outlook to manage your appointments and meetings. Using the available features helps you keep track of your own personal calendar events, and both personal appointments and meetings that you have scheduled during work hours with your coworkers. Keeping your calendar up-to-date also allows your coworkers to know when you are available and when you are not. Managing your calendar can help you manage your time more effectively and efficiently.

Do you think you will be the one sending and managing meeting requests or will you be on the receiving end of meeting requests? How do you think using Outlook will differ for those two different roles?

How do you anticipate you will use the features of the calendar, such as appointments, meetings, reminders, and printing your calendar to best manage your time?

> **Note:** Check your CHOICE Course screen for opportunities to interact with your classmates, peers, and the larger CHOICE online community about the topics covered in this course or other topics you are interested in. From the Course screen you can also access available resources for a more continuous learning experience.

8 | Working with Tasks and Notes

Lesson Time: 30 minutes

Lesson Objectives

In this lesson, you will:

- Create and manage tasks.

- Create and manage notes.

Lesson Introduction

The email messages and meeting requests that you send, receive, and manage among yourself and your recipients is fairly easy to navigate in Microsoft® Office Outlook® 2016. But how do you keep track of assignments or information that you need to remember, but don't necessarily involve other people and that are only specific to you? Outlook also provides two features to help you manage and organize these personal activities: **Tasks** and **Notes**.

TOPIC A

Create Tasks

Now that you are using Outlook to send emails, schedule meetings, and keep track of all your contacts, you might find yourself with more tasks that you have to complete. Outlook provides a handy way for you to schedule, manage, and view personal tasks that need to be completed. In this topic, you will manage your tasks in Outlook using the **Tasks** feature.

Tasks

A *task* in Outlook is an action item or activity that is assigned to you and that must be completed within a certain time frame. You can assign a task to yourself or to other people, and other people can assign a task to you. The **Tasks** view in Outlook is where you can create and manage the tasks that you assign to yourself or are assigned to you using the **Tasks** feature.

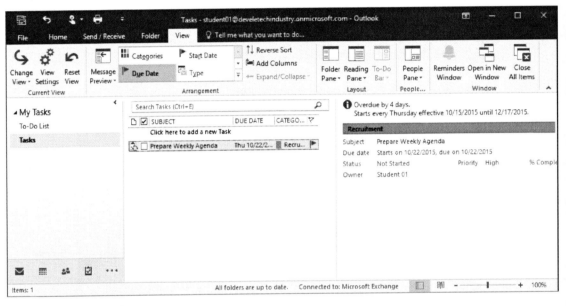

Figure 8-1: The Tasks view.

	Note: Outlook on the Web
	Using the online app, you can create, view, and edit tasks; however, if you need to assign or share tasks with others, you must use the desktop application. To view your tasks, select the **App Launcher** icon and then select the **Tasks** tile. The **Tasks** page is a simplified version of the desktop Tasks view.

| | **Note:** In this course, *Microsoft® Office Outlook® 2016: Part 1 (Desktop/Office 365™)*, tasks that you have assigned to yourself for organizational purposes are the only tasks covered. For more information about managing activities by assigning tasks to others or replying to tasks that have been assigned to you, please see the *Microsoft® Office Outlook® 2016: Part 2* course. |

Task Form

Tasks are created and managed using the task form. When you select **New Task** from the **New** command group, a blank task form opens.

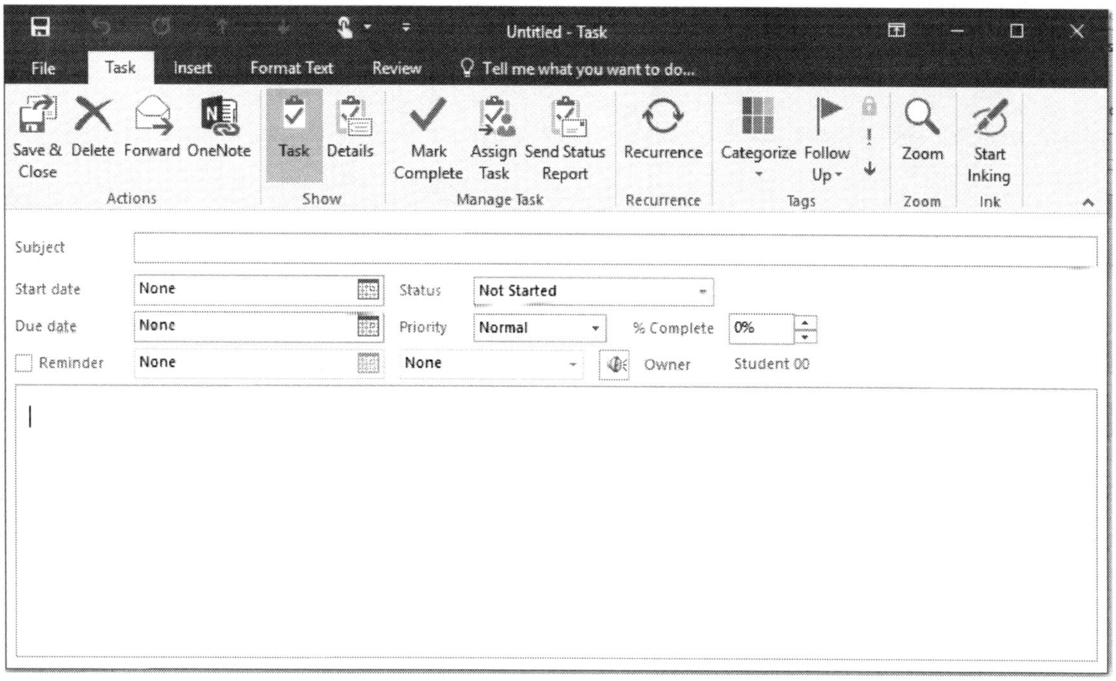

Figure 8-2: A new untitled task form.

The task form has a number of fields where you enter the necessary information about the task assignment.

- In the **Subject** field, enter a brief description of the task.
- In the **Start date** field, select the date when the task is scheduled to begin from the calendar.
- In the **Due date** field, select the date by which the task must be completed from the calendar.
- From the **Status** drop-down list, select the current status of the assignment: **Not Started**, **In Progress**, **Completed**, **Waiting on someone else**, or **Deferred**.
- From the **Priority** drop-down list, select the priority level of the assignment: **Low**, **Normal**, or **High**.
- In the **% Complete** field, use the spin boxes to select a percentage of completion for the assignment.
- If a reminder for the task is needed, check the **Reminder** check box and select a date and time from the drop-down lists for the reminder notification.
- The **Owner** field displays the owner of the task (if you assigned the task to yourself, it is your name; if the task was assigned to you by someone else, it will be the name of the person who assigned it.)
- In the message body, you can enter any specific information about the assignment.

Task Views

The tasks that are assigned to you, whether by yourself or by others, can be viewed in various locations in the Outlook interface:

- In **Tasks** view, select either the **To-Do List** or **Tasks** folder.
- In **Calendar** view, select **View→Daily Task List** and select **Normal** or **Minimized**.
- From the other Outlook views, select **View→To-Do Bar→Tasks**.
- From the **Navigation** bar, hover over the **Tasks** icon to display the **Tasks Peek**.

Within the **Tasks** view, you can view the details of the tasks assigned to you in a variety of ways. You can find the available views by selecting **Home→Current View→Change View**.

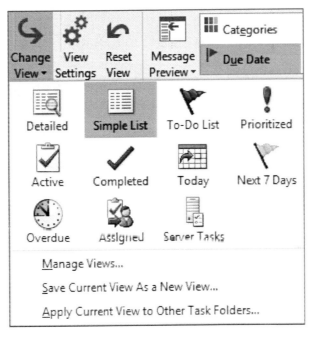

Figure 8-3: The available task views.

The following table contains the available views and their descriptions.

Task View	Description
Detailed	Displays your tasks and any of the details the task has been given, and includes the subject, status, due date, any dates it was modified, the date it was completed, the location in a folder, any color categories assigned to the task, if the task was flagged for follow up, and information that belongs in any other columns you may have added to your sort bar when customizing your environment.
Simple List	Displays your tasks as a simple list and includes the subject of the task, the due date, and any color categories or flags that have been assigned to the task.
To-Do List	Displays your tasks in the same manner that they appear in the **To-Do Bar**, and can be arranged according to their type, importance, start date, due date, or categories.
Prioritized	Displays your tasks according to the priority that has been assigned to them. Tasks are grouped by high, normal, and low priorities.
Active	Displays any of your tasks that are still active and ongoing tasks, and includes the subject, status, due date, percent complete, and any color categories or flags that have been assigned to the task.
Completed	Displays only the tasks assigned to you that have been completed, and includes the subject, due date, date completed, and any color categories or flags that were assigned to the task.
Today	Displays any tasks that are assigned for the current date, and includes the subject, due date, and any color categories or flags that have been assigned to the task.
Next 7 Days	Displays any tasks that have been scheduled for the next seven days, and includes the subject, status, due date, percent complete, and any color categories or flags that have been assigned to the task.

Task View	Description
Overdue	Displays any tasks assigned to you that are overdue/past their due date, and includes the subject, status, due date, percent complete, and any color categories or flags that have been assigned to the task.
Assigned	Displays any tasks that have been assigned to you by someone else, and includes the subject, owner, due date, status, and any flags that have been assigned to the task.
Server Tasks	Uses Microsoft Outlook, Project, and SharePoint® to synchronize and display tasks that have been assigned to members of a project team. This view includes the subject, assigned persons, status, priority level, due date, and folder location for the task.

> **Note: Outlook on the Web**
> You can sort your tasks by selecting the **Items by** menu that contains a variety of sort criteria.

Task Options

When creating and assigning a task, there are a number of options you can enable for the assignment. These options include:

- **Recurrence:** Tasks, like appointments and meetings, can be scheduled as recurring. If the assignment happens on a regular basis, such as daily or weekly, select the **Recurrence** option and configure the task to be a recurring task.
- **Regeneration:** Set the next task in a recurrence to only occur if the previous task was marked as completed.
- **Categorize:** Assign a color category to your tasks to organize and visually keep track of your tasks.
- **Follow Up:** Flag tasks for follow up to keep track of which items need further action or must be completed by a certain time.
- **Private:** Mark a task as private so that other people who may have access to your calendar cannot see the details of your task.
- **Priority levels:** Mark a task as **High Importance** or **Low Importance** to help convey the priority level of the task.

> **Access the Checklist tile on your CHOICE Course screen for reference information and job aids on How to Create Tasks.**

ACTIVITY 8-1
Creating a Recurring Task

Scenario

As a key member of the recruitment team hiring new multimedia designers for Develetech, you have been assigned many specific tasks regarding the recruitment effort. You have already scheduled weekly team meetings with the recruitment team, and you think it is a good idea to have an agenda with the items to discuss at each meeting. In fact, you want to develop the agenda the day before the weekly meeting and send it out to the team to review prior to the meeting. You can use the **Tasks** option in Outlook to manage this as a personal task for yourself.

1. Create a recurring task named **Prepare Weekly Agenda**.

   a) On the **Navigation** bar, select **Tasks**. ☑
   b) On the **Home** tab, select **New→New Task**.

   c) In the **Subject** field, type *Prepare Weekly Agenda*
   d) In the **Start date** field, select 🗓 and in the calendar, select the following **Thursday**.
   e) Observe the **Due date** field.
      It has been updated to match the **Start date**. You'll leave this due date as is.
   f) Select the **Priority** drop-down list and select **High**.
   g) On the **Task** tab, select **Recurrence**.

   ```
   ┌─────────────────────────────────────────────────────────────────────────┐
   │  Recurrence pattern                                                       │
   │  ○ Daily      ● Recur every  [ 1 ]  week(s) on                            │
   │  ● Weekly       ☐ Sunday      ☐ Monday     ☐ Tuesday    ☐ Wednesday      │
   │  ○ Monthly      ☑ Thursday    ☐ Friday     ☐ Saturday                     │
   │  ○ Yearly     ○ Regenerate new task  [ 1 ]  week(s) after each task is completed │
   │                                                                           │
   └─────────────────────────────────────────────────────────────────────────┘
   ```

   The recurrence pattern is configured based on your selected start date.

h) In the **Range of recurrence** section, select **End by** and select a date that's several months in the future.

Range of recurrence
Start: Thu 10/1/2015 ⌄   ○ No end date
                         ○ End after: 10   occurrences
                         ● End by: Thu 12/3/2015 ⌄

i) Select **OK**.

ⓘ Due in 9 days.
   Starts every Thursday effective 10/1/2015 until 12/3/2015.

Subject   Prepare Weekly Agenda

The InfoBar now displays the number of days before the task is due and the task recurrence details.

j) Select **Save & Close**.

2. View the **Prepare Weekly Agenda** task in **Tasks** view.

a) Select the new task, **Prepare Weekly Agenda** in your **Tasks** view.

◢ My Tasks   ⟨
  To-Do List   ☐ ☑ SUBJECT   ▲
  Tasks   Click here to add a new Task
                                    ☐ Prepare Weekly Agenda

The empty box to the left of the task Subject indicates that the task is not completed yet. The **Due Date**, **Categories**, and **Flag** details appear in the columns to the right.

b) Select **View→Layout→Reading Pane→Right** to display the task details.

c) Switch to the **Mail** view.

d) Select **View→Layout→To-Do Bar→Tasks**.
   The **To-Do Bar** appears at the right side of the **Mail** view and now contains a list of tasks.

e) In the **Navigation** bar, point to the **Tasks** icon to display the **Task Peek**.

3. Edit the **Prepare Weekly Agenda** task to include a reminder and a color category.

a) From the **Task Peek**, double-click the **Prepare Weekly Agenda** task.

b) In the Task window, check the **Reminder** check box. Leave the reminder date as is, but change the time to **10:00 AM**.

✓ Reminder	Thu 10/1/2015	🗓	10:00 AM ▾

c) In the **Tags** command group, select **Categorize**.

d) From the gallery, select **Recruitment**.

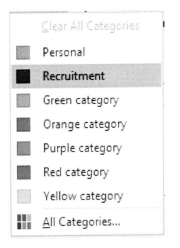

e) Observe the new category label in the Task window.

> ⓘ Due in 9 days.
> Starts every Thursday effective 10/1/2015 until 12/3/2015.
>
> **Recruitment**
>
> | Subject | Prepare Weekly Agenda |
> |---|---|

f) Select **Save & Close**.

TOPIC B

Create Notes

Technology like Outlook is constantly making it easier to communicate. But with more communication, comes more responsibilities and more information. How will you keep track of all the information that is flying around between your colleagues in emails or meetings? Outlook provides the **Notes** feature, which lets you use electronic sticky notes to keep track of information, ideas, or even meeting notes and store them in one convenient location in Outlook.

Notes

A *note* in Outlook is an electronic version of a sticky note, where you can capture small pieces of information that you need to remember and don't want to lose or forget. The **Notes** view in Outlook is where you can create and manage the notes you created using the Notes feature.

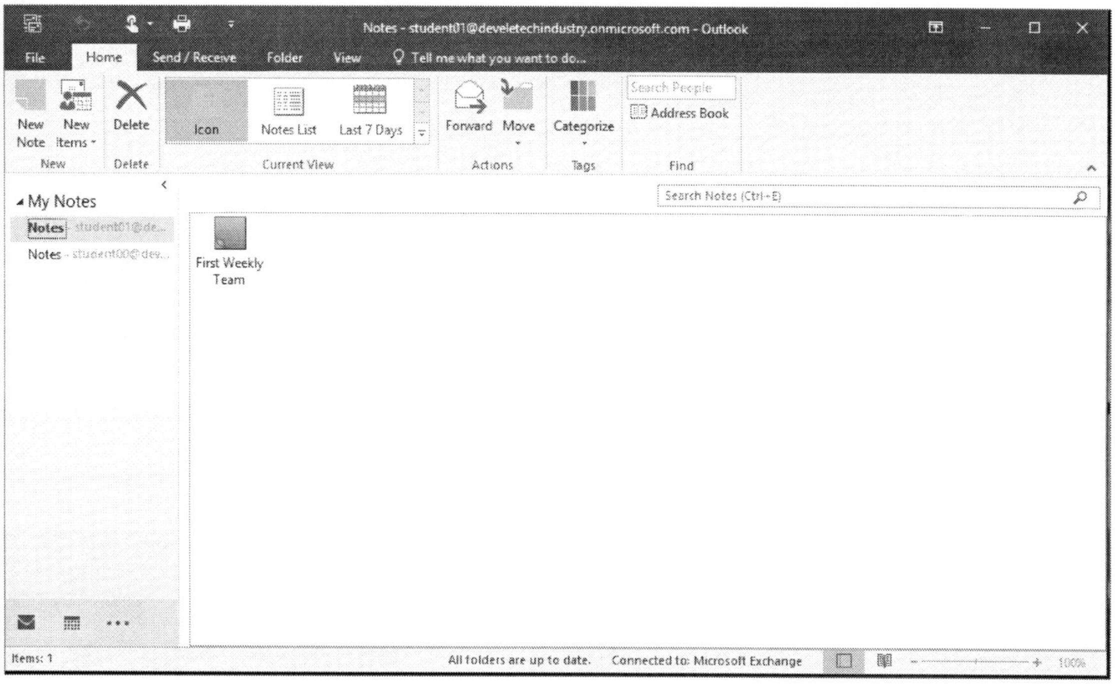

Figure 8-4: The Notes view.

> **Note: Outlook on the Web**
>
> In the online app, you need to access your notes in the **Notes** folder on your **Mail** page. From within this folder, you can view and delete notes that have been created in the desktop application; however, if you want to create or edit notes, you must do so in the desktop application.

Note Views

You can display the notes you have created in the **Notes** view in a variety of ways. These options are found on the **Home** tab in the **Current View** command group.

- **Icon** displays all of your notes as a sticky note icon. Each icon includes the first line of text in the note as the subject for context.

- **Notes List** displays all of your notes as a list. Each note in the list includes the first line of the note as a subject, the date the note was created, and any categories.
- **Last 7 Days** displays only notes that were created or changed in the last seven days in the **Notes List** view.

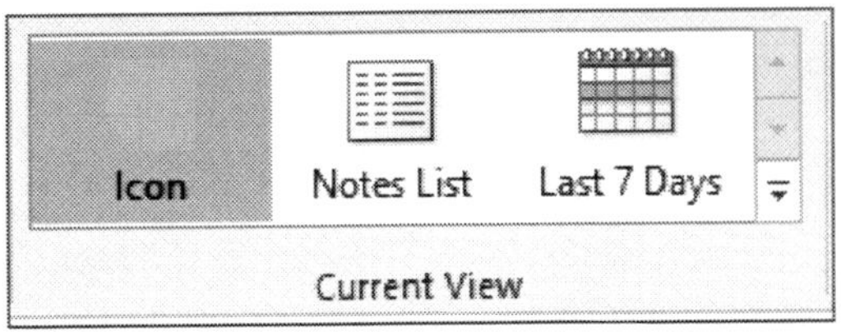

Figure 8-5: The available Notes views.

> **Access the Checklist tile on your CHOICE Course screen for reference information and job aids on How to Manage Notes.**

ACTIVITY 8-2
Creating and Modifying Notes

Scenario

Since you will be holding weekly meetings with the recruitment team that's hiring new employees for Develetech, you want to keep notes of the meetings for yourself. During your first team meeting, you'll take notes and later categorize the note so you can keep it with all the other recruitment items. After the meeting, you'll want to print the notes so everyone at the meeting has a copy.

1. Open the **Notes** view.

   a) In the **Navigation** bar, select the **More Options** icon. [···]
   b) Select **Notes**.

   > **Note:** You can change the **Navigation** bar display by selecting **More Options→Navigation Options**. From this dialog box, you can change the maximum number of visible items and the order in which items appears. If the desired button is still not visible, drag the right edge of the **Folder** pane to increase its width.

2. Create a note for your first weekly team meeting.

   a) On the **Home** tab, in the **New** command group, select **New Note**.
   A new blank sticky note appears with the date and time along the bottom edge. The blinking insertion point is ready for you to begin typing your note text.
   b) Type *First Weekly Team Meeting*

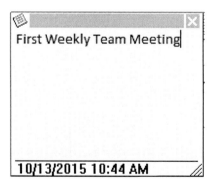

   This note title will become the name of the note.
   c) Enter the following note text under the note title and allow the text to wrap as you type. *Attendees: Angie, Martin, Jane, Alex and me. Candidates discussed: Dexter Collingsworth and Greg Shannon.*

   d) Drag the lower-right corner of the note to increase the size of the note so all of the text is visible.

   Shannon.

   10/13/2015 10:44 AM

   e) Select ☒ to close the note.

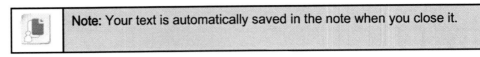

Note: Your text is automatically saved in the note when you close it.

3. Modify the current view of the **Notes** view.

   a) Observe your new note.

   Your new First Weekly Team Meeting note appears as an icon in the **Content** pane of your **Notes** view. You can open it by double-clicking the **Note** icon.

   b) In the **Current View** command group, select **Notes List**.

   Your notes are now displayed in a list with Subject, Created, and Categories as the column headings.

4. Categorize the note with the **Recruitment** color category.

   a) Make sure the that **First Weekly Team Meeting** note is selected.

   b) In the **Tags** command group, select **Categorize** and select the **Recruitment** category.

🗋	SUBJECT	CREATED ▼	CATEGORIES
	First Weekly Team Meeting	Tue 10/13/2015 10:44 A...	🟧 Recruitment

5. Print the **First Weekly Team Meeting** note.

   a) Select **File→Print**.

   b) In the **Settings** section, verify that **Memo Style** is selected.

   c) Observe the note in the preview pane.

Student 01

Modified:	Tue 10/13/2015 10:50 AM
Categories:	Recruitment

First Weekly Team Meeting
Attendees: Angie, Martin, Jane, Alex and me. Candidates discussed: Dexter Collingsworth and Greg Shannon.

You can use the **Actual Size** and **One Page** buttons in the lower-right corner of the Preview window to change the zoom so you can read the text.

d) Select the button.

6. Exit Outlook, if you will not be completing the Mastery Builders.

Summary

In this lesson, you used the **Tasks** and **Notes** features in Outlook to help you manage the more personal items you have to handle on a daily basis. Tasks help you keep track of any activities that you are responsible for completing in a timely manner, and notes can help you keep track of information or details that you might need to remember. You can also store these personal items alongside the Mail, Calendar, and Contact items you already work with on a daily basis in Outlook, allowing you to keep track of everything all in one location.

Do you think you will use the Tasks feature? If so, how?

Do you think you will use the Notes feature? If so, how?

 Note: Check your CHOICE Course screen for opportunities to interact with your classmates, peers, and the larger CHOICE online community about the topics covered in this course or other topics you are interested in. From the Course screen you can also access available resources for a more continuous learning experience.

Course Follow-Up

Congratulations! You have completed the *Microsoft® Office Outlook® 2016: Part 1* course. You have successfully used Outlook to manage the numerous aspects of communicating electronically, including managing email communications, managing calendar events, managing your contacts, and using other features like tasks and notes to keep track of your action items.

The need to share important information quickly and easily has greatly affected the ways in which we communicate. And as the technology has evolved to meet those needs, communication via email and other electronic forms has grown exponentially. As email has become *the* method of communication in the business sector, most organizations have found the need to implement a corporate mail management system such as Microsoft Outlook to handle the emails and meeting invitations sent between employees. Knowing how to use all of the basic functions Outlook provides to simplify and unify corporate communications—email, calendar invites, and contacts—will allow you to communicate with others more quickly and easily.

What's Next?

Microsoft® Office Outlook® 2016: Part 2 is the next course in this series. Part 2 of the series focuses on using the features of Outlook you learned about in Part 1, but in a more advanced manner. You will learn about advanced message options and message management, advanced contact and calendar management, and using more advanced features of Outlook like the journal, sharing folders, and managing Outlook data files.

Microsoft® 365™: Web Apps (with Skype® for Business) provides an introduction to using Office in a cloud-based environment. In this course, you will use Microsoft® Outlook® mail, Skype for Business instant messaging and online meetings, and Microsoft® SharePoint® Team Sites to work and collaborate on Office Online documents.

You are encouraged to explore Outlook further by actively participating in any of the social media forums set up by your instructor or training administrator through the **Social Media** tile on the CHOICE Course screen.

A | Microsoft Office Outlook 2016 Exam 77-731

Selected Logical Operations courseware addresses Microsoft Office Specialist (MOS) certification skills for Microsoft® Office Outlook® 2016. The following table indicates where Outlook 2016 skills that are tested on Exam 77-731 are covered in the Logical Operations Outlook 2016 series of courses.

Objective Domain	Covered In
1.0 Manage the Outlook Environment for Productivity	
1.1 Customize Settings	
1.1.1 Customize reply messages	Part 1, Topic 3-C
1.1.2 Change text formats for all outgoing messages	Part 1, Topic 3-C
1.1.3 Customize the Navigation Pane	Part 1, Topic 8-B
1.1.4 Configure views	Part 1, Topics 4-A, 6-B, 7-A, 8-A, 8-B
1.1.5 Manage multiple accounts	Part 2
1.1.6 Add an account	Part 2
1.2 Print and Save Information	
1.2.1 Print message, calendar, contact, or task information	Part 1, Topics 1-B, 6-B, 7-D, 8-A
1.2.2 Save message attachments	Part 1, Topic 3-A
1.2.3 Preview attachments	Part 1, Topic 3-A
1.2.4 Save messages in alternate formats	Part 2
1.2.5 Export messages to a data file	Part 2
1.3 Perform Search Operations in Outlook	
1.3.1 Create new search folders	Part 2
1.3.2 Search for items in messages, tasks, contacts, or calendars	Part 1, Topic 6-B; Part 2
1.3.3 Search by using Advanced Find	Part 2
1.3.4 Search by Folder	Part 2
2.0 Manage Messages	
2.1 Configure Mail Settings	

Objective Domain	Covered In
2.1.1 Set fonts for new messages and responses	Part 1, Topic 3-C
2.1.2 Create, assign, and modify signatures	Part 1, Topic 3-C
2.1.3 Create and manage rules	Part 2
2.1.4 Create automatic replies	Part 2
2.1.5 Create messages by using Quick Parts	Part 2
2.1.6 Configure junk email and clutter settings	Part 2
2.2 Create Messages	
2.2.1 Create a message	Part 1, Topics 1-B, 2-A
2.2.2 Add or remove message attachments	Part 1, Topic 3-A
2.2.3 Add Cc and Bcc to messages	Part 1, Topics 1-B, 2-A
2.2.4 Add tracking and voting options	Part 1, Topic 4-B
2.2.5 Forward and reply to messages	Part 1, Topic 1-B
2.2.6 Request a delivery or read receipt	Part 1, Topic 4-B
2.2.7 Redirect replies	Part 2
2.2.8 Flag outgoing messages for follow up, importance, and sensitivity	Part 1, Topic 5-A
2.2.9 Recall a message	Part 1, Topic 4-C
2.3 Format a Message	
2.3.1 Format text	Part 1, Topic 2-C
2.3.2 Insert hyperlinks	Part 2
2.3.3 Apply themes and styles	Part 1, Topic 3-B
2.3.4 Insert images	Part 1, Topic 3-B; Part 2
2.3.5 Add a signature to specific messages	Part 1, Topic 3-C
2.4 Organize and Manage Messages	
2.4.1 Sort messages	Part 2
2.4.2 Move messages between folders	Part 1, Topic 5-A
2.4.3 Add new local folders	Part 1, Topic 5-A
2.4.4 Apply categories	Part 1, Topic 5-A
2.4.5 Clean up messages	Part 1, Topic 5-A
2.4.6 Mark a message as read or unread	Part 1, Topic 1-A
2.4.7 Flag received messages	Part 1, Topic 5-A
2.4.8 Ignore messages	Part 1, Topic 5-A
2.4.9 Sort messages by conversation	Part 1, Topic 4-A
2.4.10 Delete messages	Part 1, Topic 1-B
2.4.11 Automate repetitive tasks by using Quick Steps	Part 2
2.4.12 Configure basic AutoArchive settings	Part 2
2.4.13 Delegate access	Part 2

Objective Domain	Covered In
3.0 Manage Schedules	
3.1 Create and Manage Calendars	
3.1.1 Create and add calendars	Part 2
3.1.2 Adjust viewing details for calendars	Part 1, Topic 7-A; Part 2
3.1.3 Modify calendar time zones	Part 2
3.1.4 Delete calendars	Part 2
3.1.5 Set calendar work times	Part 2
3.1.6 Manage multiple calendars	Part 2
3.1.7 Manage calendar groups	Part 2
3.1.8 Display multiple calendars	Part 2
3.1.9 Share calendars	Part 2
3.2 Create Appointments, Meetings, and Events	
3.2.1 Create calendar items	Part 1, Topics 7-A, 7-B
3.2.2 Create recurring calendar items	Part 1, Topics 7-A, 7-B
3.2.3 Cancel calendar items	Part 1, Topic 7-C
3.2.4 Create calendar items from messages	Part 1, Topics 7-A, 7-B
3.2.5 Set calendar item times	Part 1, Topics 7-A, 7-B
3.2.6 Set up meetings by using the Scheduling Assistant	Part 1, Topic 7-C
3.2.7 Set free or busy status for calendar items	Part 1, Topic 7-B
3.2.8 Schedule resources	Part 1, Topic 7-C
3.2.9 Set up meeting locations by using Room Finder	Part 1, Topic 7-C
3.3 Organize and Manage Appointments, Meetings, and Events	
3.3.1 Set calendar item importance	Part 1, Topic 7-B
3.3.2 Forward calendar items	Part 1, Topics 7-B, 7-C
3.3.3 Configure reminders	Part 1, Topics 7-B, 7-C; Part 2
3.3.4 Add participants	Part 1, Topic 7-C
3.3.5 Respond to invitations	Part 1, Topic 7-C; Part 2
3.3.6 Update individual or recurring calendar items	Part 1, Topics 7-B, 7-C
3.3.7 Share meeting notes	Part 1, Topic 7-C
3.3.8 Categorize calendar items	Part 1, Topics 7-B, 7-C
3.4 Create and Manage Notes and Tasks	
3.4.1 Create and manage tasks	Part 1, Topic 8-A; Part 2
3.4.2 Create and manage notes	Part 1, Topic 8-B
4.0 Manage Contacts and Groups	
4.1 Create and Manage Contacts	
4.1.1 Create a new contact	Part 1, Topic 6-A

Objective Domain	Covered In
4.1.2 Delete contacts	Part 1, Topic 6-A
4.1.3 Import contacts from external sources	Part 2
4.1.4 Edit contact information	Part 1, Topic 6-A; Part 2
4.1.5 Attach an image to a contact	Part 1, Topic 6-A
4.1.6 Add tags to contacts	Part 1, Topic 6-B
4.1.7 Share contacts	Part 2
4.1.8 Create and manage address books	Part 1, Topic 6-B; Part 2
4.2 Create and Manage Contact Groups	
4.2.1 Create new contact groups	Part 1, Topic 6-A; Part 2
4.2.2 Add contacts to existing contact groups	Part 1, Topic 6-A
4.2.3 Add notes to a contact group	Part 1, Topic 6-A
4.2.4 Update contacts within contact groups	Part 1, Topic 6-A
4.2.5 Delete contact groups	Part 1, Topic 6-A
4.2.6 Delete contact group members	Part 1, Topic 6-A

B Microsoft Outlook 2016 Common Keyboard Shortcuts

The following table lists common keyboard shortcuts available in Outlook 2016. Keyboard shortcuts that work in specific views are grouped accordingly. For a more extensive list, please refer to Outlook 2016 Help.

Function	Keyboard Shortcut
In all Outlook views	
Open Outlook 2016 Help	**F1**
Send & receive new items from the server	**F9**
Check spelling and grammar	**F7**
Undo	**Ctrl+Z** or **Alt+Backspace**
Print selected item	**Ctrl+P**
Delete selected Outlook item	**Ctrl+D**
Forward selected Outlook item	**Ctrl+F**
Reply to selected message, calendar item, or assigned task	**Ctrl+R**
Reply All to selected message, calendar item, or assigned task	**Ctrl+Shift+R**
Open the Address Book	**Ctrl+Shift+B**
Go to the Search box	**Ctrl+E**
Use Advanced Find	**Ctrl+Shift+F**
Switch to Mail view	**Ctrl+1**
Switch to Calendar view	**Ctrl+2**
Switch to Contacts view	**Ctrl+3**
Switch to Tasks view	**Ctrl+4**
Switch to Notes view	**Ctrl+5**
Create a new message	**Ctrl+Shift+M**

Function	Keyboard Shortcut
Create a new appointment	**Ctrl+Shift+A**
Create a new meeting request	**Ctrl+Shift+Q**
Create a new contact	**Ctrl+Shift+C**
Create a new contact group	**Ctrl+Shift+L**
Create a new task	**Ctrl+Shift+K**
Create a new note	**Ctrl+Shift+N**
In Mail view	
Create a new message	**Ctrl+N**
Check names	**Ctrl+K**
Send the message	**Alt+S**
Insert the current date in the message body	**Alt+Shift+D**
Display the Font dialog box	**Ctrl+Shift+P**
Insert a hyperlink (in message body)	**Ctrl+K**
In Calendar view	
Create a new appointment	**Ctrl+N**
Go to a Date	**Ctrl+G**
Show 10 days in calendar	**Alt+0** (zero)
In Contacts view	
Create a new contact	**Ctrl+N**
Find a contact	**F11**
Select all contacts	**Ctrl+A**
In Tasks view	
Create a new task	**Ctrl+N**
Accept a task request	**Alt+C**
Decline a task request	**Alt+D**

Mastery Builders

Mastery Builders are provided for certain lessons as additional learning resources for this course. Mastery Builders are developed for selected lessons within a course in cases when they seem most instructionally useful as well as technically feasible. In general, Mastery Builders are supplemental, optional unguided practice and may or may not be performed as part of the classroom activities. Your instructor will consider setup requirements, classroom timing, and instructional needs to determine which Mastery Builders are appropriate for you to perform, and at what point during the class. If you do not perform the Mastery Builders in class, your instructor can tell you if you can perform them independently as self-study, and if there are any special setup requirements.

Mastery Builder 1–1
Using Outlook Help

Activity Time: 10 minutes

Scenario

You are a new Outlook user and have run across questions about using Mail. For example, what happens to mail messages when they are deleted? Are they held in a temporary folder before they are permanently removed?

1. Use **Tell Me** to search for help on deleting Outlook items. (You can search any topic of interest to you.)

2. From the list of suggestions, select the **Get Help** option.

3. In the **Outlook 2016 Help** window, follow the links to read documents that are of interest to you.

4. Navigate through **Help** by using the buttons at the top of the window.

5. Close **Help**.

Mastery Builder 2-1
Composing and Formatting an Email

Activity Time: 10 minutes

Scenario

You want to send an email to the recruitment team with some information about another of the prospective candidates for the multimedia position, Amy Reynolds. In this mastery builder, you will compose, spell check, and format the email.

1. Open a new message form.

2. Address the message to everyone in the class with the Subject: *Amy Reynolds*.

3. In the message body, type message text to introduce Amy as a candidate.

4. Check the spelling of your message before you send it.

5. Use the **Mini** toolbar to apply **Bold** and **yellow highlights** to selected text.

6. Send the message.

Mastery Builder 3-1
Sending an Email with Attached Files and Inserted Pictures

Activity Time: 10 minutes

Data Files

C:\091058Data\Working with Attachments and Illustrations\Amy Reynolds Resume.docx

C:\091058Data\Working with Attachments and Illustrations\Amy Sample.png

C:\091058Data\Working with Attachments and Illustrations\Schedule.docx

Scenario

Continuing with the scenario in the previous mastery builder, you will send another email about the prospective candidate, Amy Reynolds. You will compose an email and then attach Amy's résumé, insert a sample of her work, and use the **Screenshot** tool to capture a picture of the interview schedule in your email.

---

1. Open a new message form.

2. Select the recruitment team members as recipients of the email.

3. Compose a message to the team about Amy's résumé and her work sample.

4. Attach Amy Reynolds' résumé to the email for your colleagues to review.

5. Insert the sample of Amy's work into the email message.

6. Use the **Screenshot** tool to capture a picture of the interview schedule and insert it in the email message.

7. Send the message.

Mastery Builder 4–1
Enabling Message Preview and Conversations

Activity Time: 10 minutes

Scenario

You want to customize your reading options to be able to quickly read and respond to your Outlook items. In this mastery builder, you will enable Message Preview and conversations for your email messages.

 Note: Please note, should you choose to do this mastery builder, you will want to disable both AutoPreview and conversations once you have completed this activity. Leaving Message Preview and conversations enabled may affect the way that other activities work in this course.

---

1. Modify the **Message Preview** options for items in your message list.

2. For your **Inbox** folder, show messages as conversations.

3. Configure how messages and message threads are displayed in a conversation.

4. Explore how Message Preview and conversations look in your Inbox.

5. Return Message Preview to the default configuration and disable conversations for your folders.

Mastery Builder 5–1
Organizing your Messages

Activity Time: 10 minutes

Scenario

You can use the many options available in Outlook to help you manage and organize your messages. In this mastery builder, you will explore using tags, flags, and folders to manage your messages.

1. Create a new color category and categorize messages or items in your Inbox using the new category.

2. Flag messages or items in your message list for follow up.

3. Use the **Clean Up** command to remove redundant emails from a folder.

4. Create a new folder and move some of your message or items from your Inbox into the new folder.

Mastery Builder 6-1
Creating Contacts

Activity Time: 10 minutes

Scenario

As the number of people you communicate with in Outlook grows, you discover that it will be more efficient for you to create contacts. Additionally, you would like to keep your work contacts separate from your personal contacts.

1. In **Mail** view, create a new contact by dragging the sender's name to the **Navigation** bar.

2. In **Contacts** view, create a new contact for yourself. Enter as much information as you want.

3. Create a new contact group named **Friends**.

4. Add yourself and your instructor to your **Friends** contact group.

Mastery Builder 7–1
Managing Recurring Calendar Entries

Activity Time: 10 minutes

Scenario

You take a kickboxing class every Wednesday from 5:30 P.M. to 7 P.M. at Bit by Bit Fitness. You want to add the class as a recurring appointment on your calendar.

You created a recurring weekly meeting with the recruitment team, but you forgot to include one of the team members on the meeting request. You need to send an update for the Weekly Recruitment Team Meeting to include one more attendee.

---

1. Create an appointment for the kickboxing class.

2. Display the time on your calendar as **Out of Office**.

3. Create a reminder for the appointment.

4. Make the appointment recurring, with **10** recurrences.

5. Categorize the appointment with the **Personal** color category.

6. Schedule the recurring appointment.

7. Verify that the kickboxing appointment appears on the following week to verify that the appointment recurs appropriately.

8. Update the **Weekly Recruitment Team Meeting** in your calendar to include one more student as a required attendee, and send the update to only the newly invited attendee.

Mastery Builder 8-1
Forwarding a Note

Activity Time: 10 minutes

Scenario

Recently, you used the **Notes** feature to take notes about what was discussed during your weekly meeting with the recruitment team. You want to forward those notes to all the members of the recruitment team.

1. Select the **First Weekly Team Meeting** note in your **Notes** list.

2. Assign the **Recruitment** category to the note.

3. Forward the note to everyone in the class, and include a message of your choice.

4. Exit Outlook.

Solutions

ACTIVITY 6-4: Viewing Contacts

2. How are the Business Card and the Card views different?

   A: The **Business Card** view displays the contact information in a formatted card layout, while the **Card** view displays the contact information in an unformatted layout with the field labels included. The **Business Card** view provides just the essential information for a contact.

4. How are the Phone and List views similar? How are they different?

   A: Both views display each contact's information in a single row. The column headings are the field labels and can be used to sort the contact list by selecting the desired field. The views are organized in slightly different ways. The **List** view groups the contacts by company name, while the **Phone** view does not group the contacts.

Glossary

address book
A repository where your contacts are stored.

appointment
An activity that you can schedule in your calendar and does not require inviting other people or using other resources, such as an online meeting or conference room. Appointments are created and managed using the Calendar view in Outlook.

attachment
A document or file that is included and sent along with your email message.

attachment preview
A feature in Outlook that allows you to preview a file that has been attached to an email message in the Reading pane.

AutoCorrect
A tool that checks for common typing errors, including spelling and grammar errors, capitalization mistakes, and other typographical mistakes. If it can determine what was intended, it will automatically correct the error; if not, it will offer suggestions for how to fix the error.

AutoText
An Outlook feature that enables you to save words or phrases that you use often and then quickly insert them into email messages from the AutoText gallery.

color categories
Colored codes that can be customized and assigned to items to visually organize and identify items that you've placed in the same category.

contact
Any person with whom you need to communicate with for business or personal reasons. Contacts are created and managed using the Contacts view in Outlook.

contextual tabs
Additional ribbon tabs that are available when an object is inserted into an email message. The contextual tab names reflect the inserted or selected object, such as Picture, Drawing, SmartArt, and Table.

conversations
An organizational tool in Outlook where all messages (sent and received) with the same subject are grouped together and can be managed as a single item. When Show as Conversations is selected, a white triangle appears to the left of the latest email message in the thread.

desktop alerts
Notifications that appear on-screen when a new Outlook item, such as an email message or meeting invitation, is delivered and arrives in your Inbox.

dialog box launchers
A small downward-arrow button located at the bottom-right corner of the command group box which, when selected, opens a

dialog box with additional features available for that command group.

email

Electronic mail, refers to electronic mail messages that can be delivered and exchanged between one sender and one or more recipients.

event

An appointment or meeting that is intended to last all day.

folders

The organizational containers in which items in Outlook are stored.

gallery

A library of all the options that are available for a specific command.

Global Address List

A list of all users, shared resources, and distribution groups that have been created and networked on the Microsoft Exchange Server for an organization.

items

Contain the information that you are viewing or modifying. Items in Outlook include email messages, calendar entries, contact information, tasks, and notes.

Live Preview

A feature in Outlook and other Office 2016 products that provides a "sneak peek" of how formatting changes will appear before they are actually applied.

MailTips

A feature that provides real-time feedback concerning the messages you are composing. While you're composing your message, Outlook and Exchange work together to determine if there are any issues that might prevent your message from being sent or delivered successfully. For example, if the recipient group was too large, a message to that effect would be displayed between the ribbon and the address fields.

meeting

An activity that you schedule on your calendar and requires inviting other people and possibly requires reserving other resources available in Outlook. Meetings are created and managed using the Calendar view in Outlook.

Message Preview

A feature in Outlook that displays the first few lines of a message in the Content pane, beneath the subject line of the message.

Microsoft Exchange Server

A mail server application that acts as the communication platform that manages and filters email messages and other types of communications, such as meeting invitations, that are sent over a network.

Mini toolbar

A floating toolbar that appears when text has been selected in the body of your Outlook message, and provides access to the formatting tools, without having to access these tools on the ribbon.

notes

An electronic version of a sticky note, where you can capture small pieces of information that you need to remember. Notes are created and managed using the Notes view in Outlook.

peeks

The feature that enables you to see a preview of the other views without having to leave the active view by pointing to the icon on the Navigation bar. For example, while in Mail view, you can point to the Calendar icon in the Navigation bar to display a Calendar thumbnail and your weekly schedule.

personal folders

Folders you can create in Outlook that are saved as personal store table (.pst) files and are stored on the local computer. When online, the folders are synchronized with the Exchange Server and are always available to you.

Policy Tips

A feature that works in the Data Loss Prevention (DLP) security layer within your organization and provides real-time feedback if the message you are composing violates an organizational policy that has been defined by your Outlook administrator. Policy Tips appear between the ribbon and the mail form.

ribbon

Common to all Microsoft Office 2016 applications, the ribbon is displayed along the top of the Outlook window and provides quick access to frequently used commands and settings. The ribbon commands are organized by tabs (such as Home, Send/Receive, Folder, and View) that contain functionally-related command groups.

ScreenTips

The small window of descriptive text that provides information about the button or action your cursor is ready to select.

secondary address books

Additional address books that you can create in Outlook, name at your discretion, and use to store your contacts.

signature

A standard closing element that can be created, personalized, and then added to the end of your email messages.

SmartArt

A tool in Outlook and other Office 2016 applications that is used to organize information in a graphical layout to more effectively communicate ideas or to convey a message.

styles

Preconfigured formatting options that can be applied to messages or other Outlook items such as font type, font color, paragraph spacing, and bulleted lists, and can be edited to suit individual needs.

task

An action item or activity that is assigned to you and that must be completed within a certain time frame. Tasks are created and managed using the Tasks view in Outlook.

Tell Me

A new feature in Microsoft Office 2016 that provides access to a specific action, command, or link to related Outlook Help documents. Located at the top of the window, you enter a keyword or phrase in the Tell Me text box and then select the desired option from the list of suggestions.

themes

Preconfigured design and formatting options that can be applied to your message to ensure consistency in all content that you create or place in the message body.

WordArt

A text-styling tool in Outlook and other Office 2016 applications that is used to insert and modify text with special effects.

Index